OPENING

a primer for self-actualization

trade edition

---

bob samples • bob wohlford

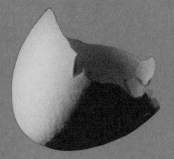

ADDISON-WESLEY PUBLISHING COMPANY
Menlo Park, California • Reading, Massachusetts
London • Amsterdam • Don Mills, Ontario • Sydney

This Book was originally published in the
ADDISON-WESLEY INNOVATIVE SERIES

Sixth printing, September 1978

ISBN 0-201-06707-2
ABCDEFGHIJ-HA-798

preface

This book is about how to remove the filters that prevent us from living more open, actualizing lives. It is not a recipe book for encounter. It is a private book intended for *in*dependent growth as opposed to the dependent growth strategies of group techniques. You do not need to have flashes of all encompassing enlightenment or expensive therapists. This book is about the way to turn everyday life into a constantly present resource for personal growth.

The approaches used in here were designed first for use with teachers, counsellors, and other adults who were "in control" of other humans. The purpose was to create more humane environments in which teaching, learning, and counselling took place. After a decade of experience it became clear that the same filters that prevented teachers and counsellors from creating actualizing environments for children were actively preventing the adults themselves from reaching actualization.

Becoming an open person isn't easy. There are hundreds of mechanisms in our lives that plead for conformity and demand a safe level of sameness. Hopefully this book will help you achieve the reality of openness, of self-actualization. It is about learning to have both the courage to reach and the vision to grow.

Bob Samples
Bob Wohlford

contents

introduction

An introduction to a book about openness should be, if nothing else, candid. So, one of the reasons I like this book is that its author, Bob Samples, is a good friend of mine. I have admired Bob and his work on the innovative frontiers of American education for many years. He is all imagination, energy, warmth and boldness—the kind of man who will probably never stop growing up. Exceptionally qualified by character, then, to try to influence the attitudes of his fellow aquarian creatures.

Another reason I like the book is that it tickles me the way Bob has wangled O.J. Harvey, Fritz Perls, Abe Maslow, Carl Rogers, Gordon Allport, Sigmund Freud (yup!), Larry Kubie, Jerry Bruner, Charles Reich, and me into the same conceptual bed. And made it appear that a good time was had by all! Now, anyone who is even casually familiar with these various authors and is willing to entertain the metaphor, is entitled to finish it according to his own polymorphous tastes. Mine I can't print, except to say that Freud came out on top. But no matter; it took a lot of courage and innocence to try to put that gang together, and Bob is the only educator I know who has enough of both to not only try it, but to pull it off. Moreover, if we didn't all have Bob's particular humanistic values and views in mind when we were writing the books he quotes, we should have.

Now, for the commercial: what kind of a book is this? It is a book about living and learning that is going to open your eyes (in more ways than one because of Bob Wohlford's dazzling graphics) and make you change. Whether you are happy with your life or bored with it; whether you like the book and accept its imperatives or dislike the book and reject its imperatives. It will have these effects because although it is a psychology book it is not constrained by the pseudo-scientific commitments to neutrality and weights of evidence which burden and befog so many others of its genre. It doesn't tell you how to live by innuendo; it tells you how to live, period. Take it or leave it. In the margin of one page of manuscript I wrote, "This is evangelistic christianity minus Judgment Day."

Not that Bob doesn't know his psychology. He does, and well. But he knows it not from back here, or up here, as a psychologist must by virtue of his training. He knows it from *in there* where living and learning and the cultivation of living and learning go on most intensely and most commonly—the public schoolroom. Bob is a teacher—of kids, of teachers, and of teachers of teachers. He has earned the right to make of psychology what he has had to make of it in order to humanize our schoolrooms. He has also earned the obligation to share these emergent views with the rest of us.

How to encapsulate these views in an introduction? In 1850 Nathaniel Hawthorne said it in *The Scarlet Letter,* "Be true! Be true! Be true! Show freely to the world, if not your worst, yet some trait whereby the worst may be inferred!" But Hawthorne had to write a heart-splitting tragedy to send his message home. Bob seems to think we can do it now without tragedies. I'd like to agree.

Richard M. Jones
Olympia, Washington

1

personal openness

Openness is an attitude. It's true that many things like life styles, ways of dealing with others, clothing choice, textbook use, evaluation procedures, etc., all can be manifested in openness . . . but it still is an attitude.

Openness is not caused by the architecture of your school or home or the way the rooms are furnished or carpeted. It is not caused by the pay you earn or the number of college units taken in school or even the act of dropping out of school. It is an attitude.

Once the attitude of openness is developed you can expect major changes to occur. Some changes will be around you in the environment called home or classroom, but most significant will be the changes in you. This doesn't mean you have to subscribe to different magazines or join new organizations, because most of the change will be inside.

You become more accepting . . . *accepting, not tolerant.* Tolerance presumes a superior or advantaged position; accepting does not. In openness hierarchies of control or power are of little importance, and usually all people and things are accepted for their own merits. Likewise, you have a fuller understanding of your own talents and potential. The result is less wasted personal energy. You also learn to accept yourself—your strengths and weaknesses become focal points for a realistic application of energy in living and teaching.

Openness is an attitude and new attitudes can be acquired and old ones changed. This book is about how openness can be achieved. It is not just a book to be read, it is a book to be done. It is not a fantasy recipe . . . it is a guidebook. It has worked for many. If it does for you, it is because you want it to.

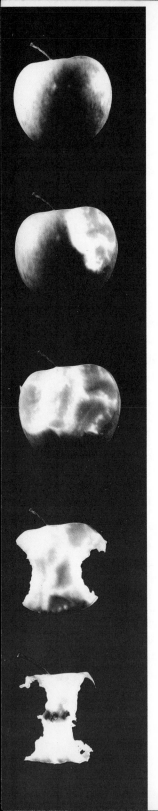

Many attitudes are reflected in what constitutes our personality. Generally we think of personality as the sum total of the characteristics that make up how we appear to be.

What this means is that our personality is structured by how various things, like our values and prejudices, are reflected in our behavior. Under normal conditions it is a tricky task to determine what constitutes a person's personality. But behavior in itself is tricky because the real issue is motivation . . . behavior can be faked.

However, when the person is under stress it is a different story. Stress tends to clarify the role of what might be called the survival motivation.

Under stress the basic characteristics of psychological and social survival patterns begin to emerge. The behaviors people begin to exhibit reflect what they really are. They exhibit the motivation they have developed in their effort to cope with life.

The personality that emerges during the stress situation is quite consistent. It is called the core personality.

What constitutes a stress situation?

Anything that happens that generates enough disruption in your comfort to make you move toward protective or survival behavior.

TRY THIS

There are twelve people coming for dinner. At the last minute, John realizes he's forgotten the mayonnaise for the artichokes. Joan volunteers to go to the grocery store.

She gets caught in the Saturday football traffic, waits five minutes to get a space in the crowded parking lot, has trouble finding the mayonnaise, then waits fifteen minutes in the "quick check" line.

The guests should be arriving now. Joan is getting nervous.

She runs out of the store just in time to be splashed by a passing truck. She makes it to the car. A large station wagon starts to angle for her parking place. She reaches in her purse. She reaches again. No Keys! Joan is locked out of her car.

The station wagon starts honking.

"Hey chickie, will you get outta there?!"

Joan's response: ???

This may cause core personality to show clearly.

One of the more pragmatic psychologists to tackle the problem of openness is O. J. Harvey at the University of Colorado. He wanted to know more about core personality so he searched out high stress professions. Guess where he went, ... you are right ... *the public school classroom*!

Of course he could have followed mothers to supermarkets, lovers to bed, and taxicab drivers to rush hour. But public school teachers are localized. Their anxieties come in the form of thirty students, sixty or more parents, and twenty administrators, as well as their own husbands, wives, lovers, children, and parents.

Using and modifying the results of his work, we recognize three categories of core personality that represent fairly consistent behavior patterns under stress. They are:

A   D   I
AUTHORITARIAN   DEPENDENCY   INTRINSIC

Each of these will be described more fully in that each has characteristics that affect openness. Remember that these categories describe *behavior under stress*. When there is no stress almost anyone can behave in any of the postures and the mix becomes quite confusing. Also, one human's stress is another's picnic. What stresses me may well be a pleasure to you ... i.e., I get uptight as a passenger in a car when the driver looks at me rather than the road.

Also keep in mind that these postures are related to *motivation*. Although we are using behaviors as an indicator, it is the motivational compulsion, the inner urge, so to speak, that determines *which* core personality you are. It's motivation, *not* behavior, that provides the real clues.

Also we use the term *value-prejudice* (or V-P) field. What we refer to here are the values and prejudices that tend to structure each person's motivation. Values and prejudices are considered to be identical psychologically but different socially. In a social sense, values have a positive connotation while prejudices are negative. This will be developed in the next chapter.

AUTHORITARIAN

Fundamentally the authoritarian sees himself as an emissary of a higher force. This may be religion, physics, phonics, or the AMERICAN WAY OF LIFE. When he is threatened and under stress, he begins to quote experts, laws, rules, commandments and other remote symbolic abstractions. The authoritarian appears to have a deep sense of history in that he is often precedent oriented.

Consider this dialog: Teacher has just finished a brilliant proof of Newton's second law (complete with colored chalk and 16 x 20 plastic coated study prints).

TEACHER: There you are! One of the brilliant proofs of humankind! (Silence is long but then broken by a bitter voice.)

STUDENT: I don't see what that crap has to do with anything!

TEACHER: You're going to the office for swearing, you know there is a rule about that. But before you go . . . I want you to know Newton was one of the greatest minds man has ever known . . . If it weren't for his genius we wouldn't be on the moon or be able to build bridges and cars the way we do. He was one of the true geniuses of all times. (Fills out detention pass while talking.)
And just in mechanics alone . . . . But obviously you can't have the capacity to understand his genius.

7

People tend to create stress for other people. Authoritarian core personalities are usually rather blasé about others until "those people" reject the authority which the authoritarian represents.

When someone creates a stress . . . that is, challenges his authority, this core personality type usually attacks from the rear. Here is how it works:

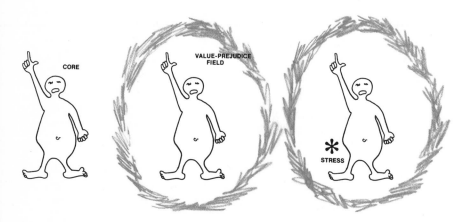

The authoritarian core personality has a distant, remote, and abstract value prejudice field. There is little or no inner orientation in this person. When authoritarians are under stress, they generally deal with it by invoking authority. What this means is that authoritarians ignore the source of the stress at first. They go to their authority to get reaffirmed before they attack.

Authoritarians are true believers. They feel they have been placed upon the earth to speak for a higher cause. There is no consistency to their causes, but there is consistency to their indignation. Authoritarians, whether they be Dodger fans, bullfighters, priests, or experts in physics, respond to stress with shock and disbelief. Their values and prejudices are a religion; disbelievers are doomed to hell—and authoritarians know where hell is.

This personality type almost always comes from environments of strict and enforced regimentation. In these unyielding social and family settings, they have two choices: to become true believers or to become revolutionaries. Whatever the choice, this personality type becomes consumed by the authoritarian ethic. True believers die to keep it. Revolutionaries die to destroy it.

This personality is exemplified in the United States by the Puritan ethic. Our forefathers sought shelter in the new land as revolutionaries escaping the dogma of England and its religions. They endured incredible hardships because of their "true belief." The ethic and the personality spread West. It followed the wagon trains over the bodies of buffalos and Native Americans. Now it is resurrected on TV and movie screens by the countless showdowns and shootouts that give us the final image of the authoritarian as a latter day Marlboro man.

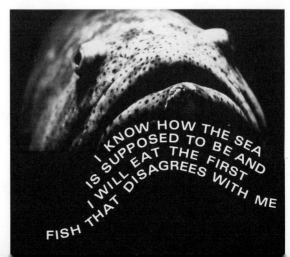

I KNOW HOW THE SEA IS SUPPOSED TO BE AND I WILL EAT THE FIRST FISH THAT DISAGREES WITH ME

DEPENDENCY

Dependency core personalities think of themselves as helpers or users of people. Although they, like the authoritarians, may invoke and use authority, they do so for the purpose of manipulating people. They are focused on a more emotionally based relationship with others. They have emotionally oriented *want* systems; they *want* people to need them or they want to express their need for others.

Try this:
BOY AND GIRL SITTING IN FRONT OF TV. GIRL IS READING.

BOY: . . . Linda . . .
GIRL: Hmmm?
BOY: Do you love me?
GIRL: . . . Sure, Billy.
BOY: A lot?
GIRL: (now distracted) SURE BILLY . . . WHY?
BOY: Well . . . if you really loved me, you would get me a beer.
GIRL: (looks strangely at boy)

The dependency core personality is a bit more direct than the authoritarian. At least this is true in motive if not execution. Rather than being an emissary for a greater power, the dependency core lives to manipulate others or to be manipulated. Dependency cores may, however, use any mechanism known to do the job. They may rail at you as an authoritarian or curl up like an indulgent puppy, but in any case they are trying to control or be controlled by others.

Unlike the authoritarian, the dependency core personality has the value-prejudice field closely attached to their emotional essence. Thus, dependency people become more personally involved in the process of "getting one's way."

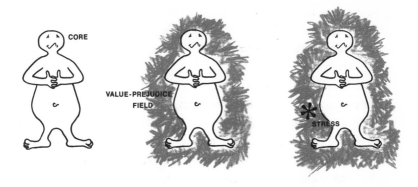

In the dependency core personality the value-prejudice field is so close to the person that it includes nearly all the people who are present. Stress always seems to originate in other people. Thus dependency cores seem to be vulnerable at all times because they focus so permanently on others. When a real stress situation occurs, they concentrate on the person that they feel is to blame. Almost at once they begin to manipulate that person. They will use any kind of manipulation—intellectual, emotional or sexual—but they will manipulate.

The dependency cores compulsively look outside themselves as do the authoritarians. If someone is wrong it is someone else's responsibility, although to manipulate others into roles of greater accommodation the dependency core may *pretend* to be at fault. Remember, it is the dependency focused motivation that makes them exhibit the behavior that nurtures the greatest manipulative control.

The dependency core personality seems consistent with what scholars have called the technocratic ethic, in other words, the assembly line mentality. You do your job so I can do mine. An expected kind of dependency comes from such an attitude. It forces us upon each other, and it isn't long before the rules get snarled. People begin to think they must obligate others in the act of living their own lives. They feel unable to make choices, because they feel that the choices have been made already.

If the Marlboro man is the image of the authoritarian, then the pro football player symbolizes the dependency core personality. Strong dependency on others and a "let's work together" attitude become "teamwork" on the playing field. Those who prefer to do athletics alone—swimmers, surfers, skiers, snorklers—seem somewhat deviant.

HURRY UP, TAMMY, WE'LL BE LATE FOR CAMPFIRE GIRLS AND THEN I'VE GOT TO GET YOU TO BALLET. WOW I MUST LOVE YOU TO DO ALL THIS FOR YOU

INTRINSIC

The fundamental characteristic of intrinsic core personalities is that they accept the responsibility for their actions. This does not mean that they are incapable of exhibiting both authoritarian or dependency behavior but that the motivational configuration is different. Generally the percentage of time they do so is quite low and, when questioned about their behavior, intrinsic core personalities always internalize and accept personal responsibility for what they do. Also what constitutes stress is usually much closer to the individual than in previous cases.

A mother is talking to a child who is playing with a camera.

MOTHER: Hey, I'm glad you're getting turned on to taking pictures.

CHILD: I hope I don't break it.

MOTHER: That's pretty hard to do and, after all, you're *ten* now (smiles).

CHILD: What's this?

MOTHER: Try it . . . (camera clicks)

CHILD: Did I take a picture?

MOTHER: Not really, there is no film in the camera.
(Child fumbling around opens the back of the camera, looks up with shock as there is an un-rewound roll of color film that has just gotten ruined.)

CHILD: Oh Mommy, I am sorry.

MOTHER: Hon, it's not your fault. *I* thought I emptied it.

Intrinsic core personalities, like both other groups, tend to have a highly developed value-prejudice (V-P) field to which they resort under stress. However the fundamental difference is that the field is primarily internalized. Like the scientist who disagrees with a colleague's theories, intrinsic cores generally believe they have simply used the same data differently. They take the posture of saying you do what it is that you believe in and they will do what they believe. They cannot say you *are* wrong. They can only say they *believe* you are wrong.

It is easy to think of the intrinsic core as being selfish, inner directed, and mentally perturbed. But to do so is to miss the point. Intrinsic personalities realize that they choose and/or maintain their own value-prejudices. Like authoritarians, they may be strong believers in a god, or a political party, or yoga. But seldom will intrinsic personalities question your morality if you disagree with them. Like dependency personalities, they may be passionate team players, legislators, or family members. But their sense of cooperative obligation is chosen rather than obediently followed. Intrinsic personalities are motivated to communicate their being, rather than coerce your being.

Intrinsic core personalities are no less committed to issues or positions of conviction than others. It is just that they internalize the responsibility for their motives and when confronted by disagreement their fundamental posture is to accept the responsibility and not externalize toward authority or manipulation. Both authoritarian and dependency *defer* the responsibility. In a strong sense the higher the outside stress the more responsibility the intrinsic-core person behaves with. Both authoritarian and dependency cores tend to disintegrate under high stress while the intrinsic cores become more stable. The reason for this is that intrinsic cores accept the responsibility for their motivation instead of feeling they are the victim of outside forces as do authoritarian and dependency.

The apparent implosion of values and prejudices from the external role of the authoritarian, to the internal role of the intrinsic, has persuaded many that intrinsics are navel-gazing recluses. Not so. The intrinsic core personality is a kind of transition state. Once aware and fully sensitized to their own choices of values and prejudices, intrinsic people quickly return to the normal patterns of life. They continue teaching, parenting, legislating, farming; but they do so with the inner competence derived from knowing it is their choice. If intrinsics are unhappy with their choices, they plan for new ones.

I DON'T KNOW HOW I GOT INTO THIS, BUT I GUESS IT'S TIME TO CONSIDER SOME ALTERNATIVES

These personality postures have internal differences that are important as well. The first two, authoritarian and dependency, have clearly defined positive and negative qualities that are often in opposition.

All of the traditions and methods of the past are virtues for the +A. They choose the history that is successfully related to their contemporary situation and make it their cause.
GO!. . GO! STATUS-QUO!

To the -A everything that agrees with social preferences is *wrong*. They want to destroy the accepted institutions and turn history around.
BURN THE *#(#* DOWN!

The +D manipulates others for success and then blames them if success isn't reached. These people are users and have excuses close at hand to explain everything away. ALL THE WORLD IS GRASS AND I AM A LAWN MOWER.

The -D maintains the posture of wanting to be manipulated. They tend to credit others for their successes and blame themselves for failures.
I AM A PAWN ON THE CHESSBOARD OF LIFE.

The intrinsic core personality is really a resting place, or a transition point. It is the focus of awareness that accompanies the acceptance of full responsibility for one's values and prejudices. But more than that its existence precedes accepting the responsibility for being with others and a part of humankind. The intrinsic marks the end of the hollow human. The quotation on the next page fits well the beginnings of the intrinsic.

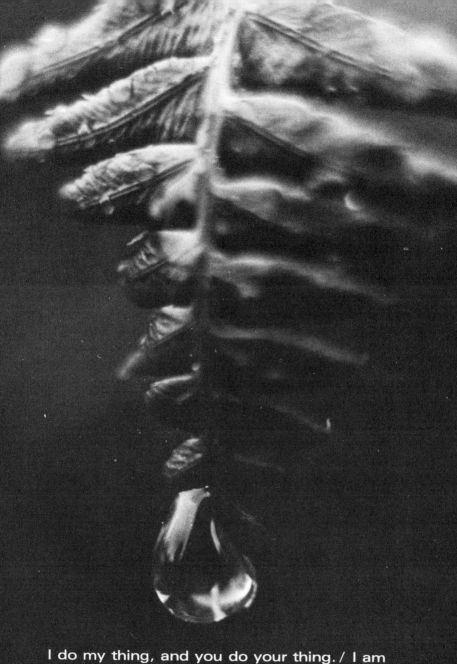

I do my thing, and you do your thing. / I am not in this world to live up to your expectations / And you are not in this world to live up to mine. / You are you and I am I, / And if by chance we find each other, it's beautiful / If not, it can't be helped.

Make no mistake. . . . .our value-prejudices are dear. . . .

Openness is easier if you have an intrinsic core personality. In pages to come we will develop strategies and tactics to accomplish movement toward an intrinsic core.

The reason we are emphasizing openness and the intrinsic core personality is because intrinsic humans have fewer hang-ups. They spend less human energy in evaluation and judgment and more in acceptance and fulfillment. They have the capacity to effectively get off of their own back and also not weigh heavily on others.

The main purpose for this book's focus is that we have never met humans who did not want to spend less of their human energy in anguish, frustration, anger, and helplessness. There are thousands of sources of these feelings outside each of us . . . but inside each of us is the mechanism to filter away these outside influences. To achieve this openness we must develop more understanding about the value-prejudice structure.

values and prejudices

12. Seagulls are: (choose one)
    a. beautiful
    b. dirty
    c. cruel
    d. graceful
    e. none of the above

Figure it out for yourself. Here are some of the responses to the question, How do you feel about seagulls?

GRACEFULSCAVENGERSDIRTY
CRUELNOISYNASTYBEAUTIFUL
STRONGNECESSARYMEANFUNNY
UGLYTIMIDSPOOKYPLAYFUL
WILDSTUPIDCUNNING
FEARFULVIOLENTCLUMSY

All of these words are expressions of an evaluative sort about seagulls. It is sometimes surprising how subtle evaluation really is. Using male or female pronouns often expresses value prejudices of an evaluative sort. For instance, elementary school teachers are often referred to as "she" or "her" while doctors and lawyers are nearly always spoken of as "he" or "him." Such value-prejudices are so much a part of language patterns that it is often overlooked. Although we will talk much more about evaluation later, let it suffice to say that evaluation is the operational expression of the value-prejudice field each of us possesses. All of the expressions used to describe the seagulls are hints about the value-prejudices regarding seagulls that the person saying them has.

Ordinarily values are thought of as the positive qualities that affect our judgment in making decisions about how we live our lives. Prejudices are usually thought to be the negative influences in decision making.

We are hyphenating value-prejudice because regardless of the sign, positive or negative, both tend to strongly influence the guidelines each of us possess in living our lives. Also, we do not think that values and prejudices are very different. If you do, then decide which of the following are statements of value and which are statements of prejudice.

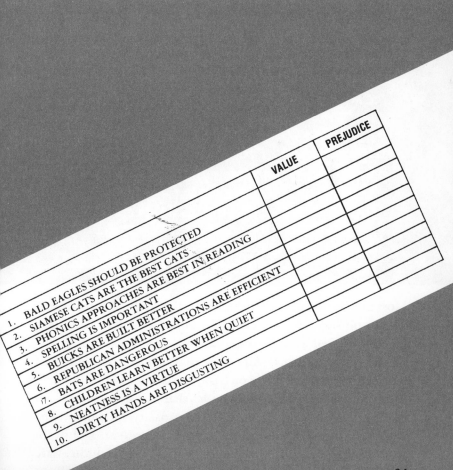

	VALUE	PREJUDICE
1. BALD EAGLES SHOULD BE PROTECTED		
2. SIAMESE CATS ARE THE BEST CATS		
3. PHONICS APPROACHES ARE BEST IN READING		
4. SPELLING IS IMPORTANT		
5. BUICKS ARE BUILT BETTER		
6. REPUBLICAN ADMINISTRATIONS ARE EFFICIENT		
7. BATS ARE DANGEROUS		
8. CHILDREN LEARN BETTER WHEN QUIET		
9. NEATNESS IS A VIRTUE		
10. DIRTY HANDS ARE DISGUSTING		

If you had trouble with the quiz don't feel bad, most people do . . . . It is quite difficult to separate values from prejudices in practice. Most often we inherit both from the same sources . . . authority or experience.

My parents, my church, my society, and my friends generally have sculptured the value-prejudices I possess and operate by; they first appear difficult to alter without a good deal of personal effort. However evidence is mounting that value-prejudices can be changed when whoever wants to change them becomes aware what they are. Consider the following statements made by one teacher over a two-month period.

SEPTEMBER 17, 1969

IT IS IMPORTANT TO GRADE STUDENTS CAREFULLY AND OBJECTIVELY SO THE STUDENTS CAN GAIN CONFIDENCE IN THEIR PROGRESS. THAT'S HOW YOU CAN BEST DEVELOP SELF-ESTEEM IN THE KIDS.

NOVEMBER 29, 1969

THE ONLY WORTHWHILE GRADE A STUDENT CAN GET IS THE ONE HE GIVES HIMSELF. I CAN NO LONGER ASSUME MY ADMINISTRIVIAL EVALUATION CRITERIA CAN HONESTLY REPRESENT ANY KID.

Most motivational theory is based on the study of animals that do not possess what we can call human will. Rats, cats, and pigeons as well as some other laboratory animals are far less willful than humans. Add this to the fact that much of motivation theory is based on basic needs like food, water, and pain avoidance, and it is no wonder that it is so inadequate in dealing with humans who have the capacity to choose. The words above written by the teacher represent a shift·in attitude that was a willful choice. Values and prejudices are inherited from many sources but retained as an act of will.

CREATIVE ACTIVITY CANNOT FLOURISH IN AN ATMOSPHERE OF REDUCTIONISM AND DETERMINISM

Colin Wilson

TWO FEATURES OF AUTONOMOUS MAN ARE PARTICULARLY TROUBLESOME . . . HIS FREEDOM AND DIGNITY

B. F. Skinner

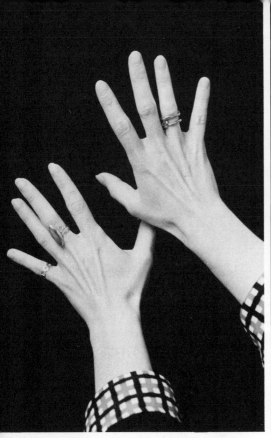

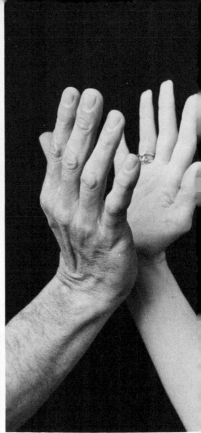

OPERATIVE

Operative values are those that are most important in living my day-to-day existence in terms of myself. My clothes, my music, my food choices, and all the other personal nuances of my value-prejudices are in this category. These are best fitted into the notion of values important in the system of

CONCEIVED

These values are the values I possess that I feel, think about, and then am compelled to communicate to others. I use these to set up a sphere of comfort that includes others. This suite of values is designed to include the system

ME-ME

ME-YOU

OBJECTIVE

Objective values are the values that represent consensus positions of large groups of like-minded people. They are global, social, and affect me mostly in that they are abstracted and codified. These are included in the system

ME-THEM
or ME-IT

WHEN CARL ROGERS, A LEADING HUMANISTIC PSYCHOLOGIST, FIRST PUT THIS CATEGORY SYSTEM TOGETHER, HE WAS THINKING ABOUT MATURE INDIVIDUALS. IT SEEMS TO US TO REPRESENT A SCHEME IN WHICH THE MATURE PERSON DIFFERENTIATED BY HIS ACTION THE VALUE SPHERES.

THE FANTASY OCCURRED TO US THAT THE IMMATURE PERSON MIGHT COMPULSIVELY INSIST ON OPERATIVE VALUES BECOMING OBJECTIVE, THAT IS IF I WERE IMMATURE AND/OR INSECURE I MIGHT INSIST ON YOU WEARING THE SAME CLOTHES THAT I DO.

OR, IN OTHER WORDS, I COULD INSTITUTIONALIZE MY OPERATIVE VALUES — CLOTHES CHOICE — INTO AN OBJECTIVE MODE BY MAKING THEM INTO A *DRESS CODE.*

OPERATIVE CONCEIVED OBJECTIVE

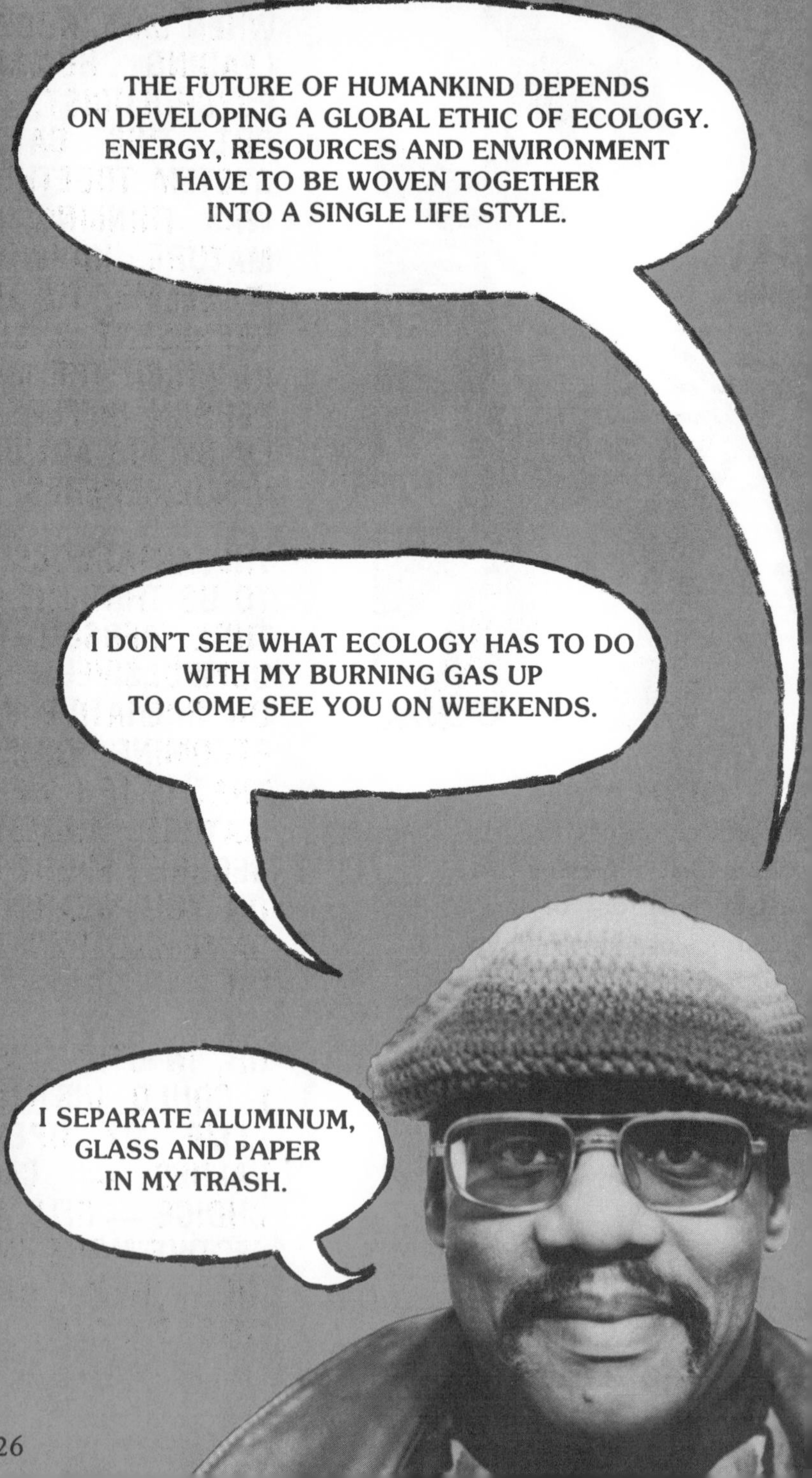

The authoritarian core personality when under stress is most comfortable in objective values. His prejudices are toward abstract consensus postures. He is, as we said earlier, a spokesman for a higher authority. He defers to authority when questioned. Often a zealot, he wants you to agree with him for a higher cause. If you do not, the blame is yours and he simply considers you inferior.

AUTHORITARIAN

The dependency core personality tends to turn his value-prejudices into conceived value postures. He lives for manipulation; thus the me-you posture is vital. He defers to objective values only to use in the process of manipulating others. Although he may invoke objective values he feels a real sense of personal loss if you do not agree with him.

DEPENDENCY

The intrinsic core personality tends to make all values operative. He has strong conceived and objective value postures but no sense of deference. He accepts operationally the responsibility for all value-prejudice postures. He may well be disappointed if he fails to communicate a belief to you but internalizes the responsibility.

INTRINSIC

One of the most pressing problems about value-prejudices is not related to whether or not they can be changed but to the general apathy we have in not examining them.

There is no magic in the process of value-prejudice clarification other than honesty. One can easily fake honesty to others, but it is impossible to fake it to yourself. Try this. Respond to the following statements either in your head or in the space provided.

YES
+

NO
FEELING
-- o

NO
—

1) Kids should make decisions about school

2) Kids should go to church

3) Kids should have pets

4) Kids should be called "children"

5) Love is a basic need

6) Honesty is the best policy

7) Never lie to a parent

8) Grades should be objective

9) Evolution should be taught

There are at least a dozen ways to respond to the statements in the last quiz, and only one is honest. If you knew the sheet was going to be "graded" by us, you might have stated your responses so that it appeared that you were a proponent of openness. If it were to be "graded" by your boss or someone you live with, you might have stated responses that agree with accepted policies. If you are honest, you answered it for yourself.

The best way to check out the pressure of value-prejudice presence is to check out your own emotions and what calls them into play.

Also check yourself out when you call *other* people's emotions into play.

GORDON ALLPORT in his classic book called *The Nature of Prejudice* wrote a chapter about traits due to victimization. In this chapter Allport dealt with the way people who are prejudiced against tend to behave. The following list modified from Allport indicates these traits.

PREJUDICIAL DISCRIMINATION

FRUSTRATION

AS DEALT WITH BY **EXTROVERTS**	AS DEALT WITH BY **INTROVERTS**
SUSPICION	GROUP DENIAL
OBSESSIVE CONCERN	WITHDRAWAL
SLYNESS	PASSIVITY
CUNNING	CLOWNING
IN-GROUP FORMATION	SELF-HATE
OUTWARD PREJUDICE	IN-GROUP AGGRESSION
AGGRESSION	SYMPATHY WITH VICTIMS
REVOLT	STATUS STRIVING
STEALING	NEUROTICISM
COMPETITIVENESS	
REBELLION	
ENHANCED STRIVING	

Without much imagination this can be seen as a check-list for the way children generally behave in the presence of adults. CHILDREN ARE AS A GROUP CONSTANTLY SUFFERING PREJUDICE FROM ADULTS. ALSO IT IS A CLEAR-CUT CHECKLIST FOR THE WAY SOME WOMEN BEHAVE IN THE PRESENCE OF MEN. If I were to rank groups against whom prejudice is most flagrantly shown, I would rank children highest, women second, and racial minorities third, in terms of consistency.

Openness is an attitude or, if you will, a value-prejudice posture that is focused on practices and behaviors that originate from acceptance as opposed to rejection. Value-prejudices that *exclude* tend to inhibit openness. Value-prejudices that are *accepting* tend to nurture openness.

MAN: Babe . . .
WOMAN: Yes?
MAN: I saw an old friend in Boston . . .
WOMAN: How was she?
MAN: How did you know it was a woman?
WOMAN: Do you think you would be so shy about telling
         me about a man?
MAN: . . . I guess not.
WOMAN: I would rather not hear any more right now.
MAN: O.K.
WOMAN: I'm glad we love each other.
MAN: Me too, . . . It's the best thing I've known.
WOMAN: But obviously not the only thing you've known!

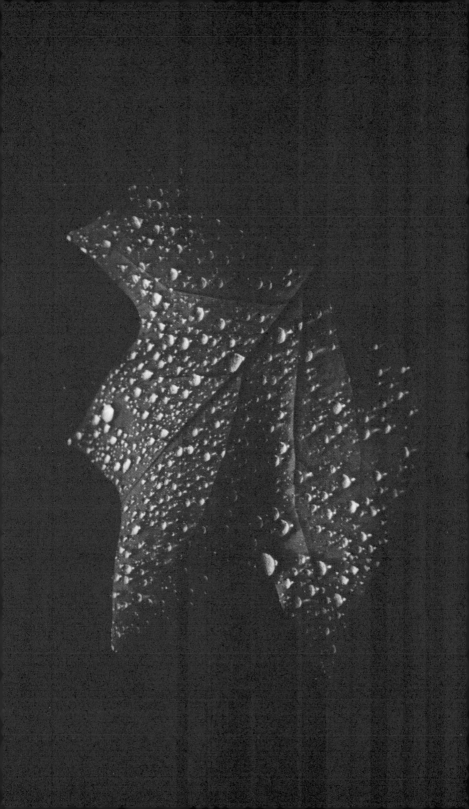

The purpose of these last two chapters has been to sensitize the reader to two key elements in openness. The personality posture and the access routes to that personality . . . the value-prejudiced field.

My value-prejudice field is the mortar that holds my personality together. I can change my value-prejudices . . . but first I must know what they are. These chapters provided a chance to paint a broad-brush portrait of categories of personality. Secondly, some detail was povided about value-prejudices which act as the stabilizing influence on my core personality. In Chapter Four we will get to actualization, but the next chapter is another construct vital to the whole process . . . the preconscious. Each of our minds is capable of being far more than it is. The preconscious helps provide access to an arena of our mind that will help soften up the hold that our value-prejudices have on us and thus allow movement toward different core personality postures.

As far as openness is concerned the psychology of prejudice and personality characteristics is far more relevant than the psychology of learning.

If I choose
to fly ~
I must risk
Finding the Sun

3

The preconscious is the meadowland of creativity. It is the birthplace of ideas in each human being that has ever lived. It is a persistent domain of experience that withstands social and philosophical pressures that, in the western tradition, are designed to suppress, ridicule, and even systematically delegitimize its existence.

It wasn't long ago that people who exhibited creative talent were considered to be a bit weird. In fact, neurosis was considered to be a necessary condition of creativity. Myth had artists, performers, writers, and many others so full of idiosyncracies that they were accepted as being reasonably deviant. Often the celebrity would behave in such a way that his posture was exaggerated simply because he was in the public eye.

The jumping into swimming pools and traffic violations or general disorderly behavior seemed amplified and magnified by the high visibility of notoriety and fame.

In terms of the creative myth, Van Gogh was awarded a certain kind of madness as exhibited by his desperate act of cutting off his ear and eventually ending his life. The myth-makers traced his growing madness through his paintings and cited a progressive loss of faculties. Ophthalmologists, when viewing his work in a chronological order, see evidence for progressive glaucoma. Result . . . was Van Gogh's creativity the product of his mental despair or was his mental despair the result of the realization of an incredible human fear . . . advancing blindness? Few humans, artists particularly, could be expected to behave well with such awareness.

FREUD

Sigmund Freud provided most of the theoretical impetus to this distorted view of creativity. Much of his work focused on a somewhat negative view of the human condition in which a warring world of battle lived within the psyche. He saw the irrational, unconscious, animal instincts fiercely resisting the rational processes of the human mind and spirit. The genius of his recognition of the unconscious led him to insights that changed the course of psychology. He worked with people with deep psychic illnesses, and pursuing the origins of these illnesses provided Freud with the realization that there was more to man than the rational mind processes championed by Aristotle.

He believed neurotic or aberrant behavior to be irrational and thus not reasonable. Reason was the epitome of the properly functioning intellect. The mind was supposed to be reasonable. Any deviation from internally consistent reasoning was considered a sign of mental illness. This view held that humans were destined to use their minds for logical acts of reason. Only the baser, more instinctive, acts tended to interfere with that reasoning capacity. He believed that neurosis increased in direct proportion to the dominance of unconscious processes in the psychic style of humans. Consider the three profiles on the next page.

Profile of a rationally dominant person whose "thinking" exhibits a high degree of orderliness and reasoning.

Profile of a person whose thinking is equally dominated by unconscious uncontrollable thought processes.

Profile of a person who exhibits high degrees of neurosis as his thinking is controlled by high degrees of irrational unconscious dominance.

RATIONAL
CONSCIOUS
THOUGHT
PROCESSES

IRRATIONAL
UNCONSCIOUS
THOUGHT
PROCESSES

INCREASING INCIDENCE OF NEUROSIS

Henri Rousseau: The Sleeping Gypsy 1897
The Museum of Modern Art, New York; gift of Mrs. Simon Guggenheim

Was that all there was to it? . . . Man's mind against his animal instincts. Not only the historical prejudices of western man but now the psychological prejudices toward the religion of rationality had been verbalized. The concept of Mind became distorted by many as being all that mattered.

Out of the work of Freud and dozens of his successors came the practice of psychiatry that was focused upon the removal of those conditions in the corridors of men's minds that resulted in behavior that was considered to deviate from the rational, intellectual, and explainable in man's experience. Dreams and pre-intellectual experience were primarily accepted as being indicative of the animalistic in man. Sexuality and a variety of biologically based functions became the representative causes of neurotic behavior in Freudian interpretations of deviant behavior. Thus, a myopic kind of pessimism about the human condition crept into the theoretical framework of how the human mind works.

Is the glass—
half full
or half empty?

A DREAM IS A WISH
YOUR HEART MAKES

In Walt Disney's remake of the classic fairy tale *Cinderella*, a song writer came up with one of the many indicators that things were in reality quite different. In a medium far from the film-makers access routes to everyday man, Lawrence Kubie, a psychologist and psychiatrist, began toying with the dichotomous models of Freud. Kubie saw a sort of demilitarized zone between the Rational Conscious processes and the Unconscious processes (Ratcon vs. Uncon).

This zone Kubie called the Preconscious processes (Precon) and he saw it as an accessible reservoir of human experience. It was a blend of tacit knowings, meaningful but not formalized experience, hunches, intuitions, and fantasy relations. It differs from the Uncon in that it *is* accessible by methods other than deep therapy techniques. Richard Jones, a psychologist and a colleague of the father of self-actualization, Abraham Maslow, took a lead from Kubie. With an optimistic gleam in his eye, he moved quickly into relating the preconscious processes of dreaming and creativity.

Jones called dreams "preconscious picture shows." He brought to the attention of many the functional, widely experienced realm of dreaming. Dreams are personal statements made to an individual by his preconscious processes. They provide a common expression to those having them that their preconscious is alive, well, and, with a bit of concentration, accessible.

42

Effective surprise . . . but where do surprises come from? Could it be that the surprising results of creative involvement and creative connections come from rationally assessing the conditions involved in the Creative act?

Not so . . . said so many researchers that the thesis was hard to ignore. Invention was capricious and impossible to predict but it *could* be encouraged.

Poincaré, while visualizing fireflies landing on a bush, discovered a complex interdependency in mathematics that became known as the Fuchsian Functions.

CREATIVITY IS EF

Playfulness is more important than rationality in creating the conditions for effective surprise. Rationality is important in anchoring it but the seedling is born of play.

The most beautiful and profound emotion that man can experience is a sense of the mystical . . . it is the dower of all true science.
Albert Einstein

CTIVE SURPRISE

JEROME BRUNER

Freud believed creativity to be rooted in neurosis. So his solution was the one shown on page 39. That is, the more one's unconscious dominated, the more mad one would become. Kubie thought this scheme could not work, so he introduced the preconscious. Let's compare the same three people in Freud's scheme and in Kubie's scheme.

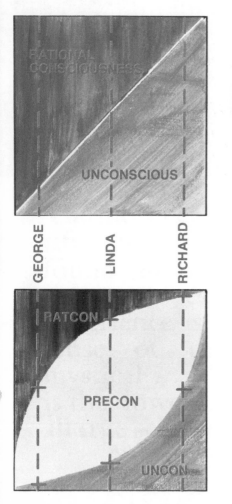

In Freud's interpretation the most creative would be the most neurotic . . . in other words, RICHARD. The least creative (most rational) would be GEORGE. LINDA was somewhere in between. Freud's focus on the unconscious related to his emphasis on illness in mental processes. Those whose mental processes were the least predictable were considered bizarre and thus mentally ill.

Kubie, on the other hand, felt that often the unpredictable surprise behavior was the product of a healthy mind. His research was aimed at showing that high neurosis interfered with creativity.

Kubie would see the same three people as shown to the left. LINDA, who had most access to the preconscious, was the most likely to be creative, RICHARD would be much less so, and—the surprise of the system—GEORGE would also be very low on creativity.

In the past, we didn't know certain vital things about how the mind works. However, recent research has shown that very different mental processes are operating in human minds. One set of operations is rational, logical, and linear. The other set is metaphoric, analogic, and intuitive.

Robert Ornstein, David Galin, and others have shown that the rational and metaphoric minds actually reside in different sides of the brain. In most people, the rational mind is in the left cerebral hemisphere, while the right hemisphere is the the place where the metaphoric mind engages the preconscious process.

In work we have done, it is becoming more apparent that the metaphoric mind is the birthplace of creativity. However, there seems to be a strong prejudice against certain forms of creativity in our society. Daydreaming, night dreaming, changing one's mind, not following rules, coming to decisions on the basis of intuition—these are all considered improper or "weird." So it is no wonder that creative people are constantly bombarded with statements like:

> "Pay attention."
> "That is a stupid dream, it makes no sense at all."
> "Make up your mind for heaven's sake!"
> "Hey you cheated! You can't play invisible hopscotch!"
> "That decision makes no sense, you must have a better reason than it feels good."

When pursued compulsively, ratcon, or rational consciousness, can become a neurosis. In many ways, our society is
slanted toward rational neurosis. For instance, prejudice
against women's intuition has been a chauvinist game for
hundreds of years. Yet, even though we have used heavy doses
of rationality for centuries, the problems facing us today are
strikingly similar to those of the past. And the solutions are
just as elusive.

Could it be that the real solutions lie in the preconscious
meadowland of the right cerebral hemisphere? If so, it might
be time to celebrate the intuitive. Perhaps men should start
listening to women, and both should start listening to
children:

KARI (four years old): Bobi?

BOB: Yes, Kari.

KARI: Can I go to bed now?

BOB: Sure . . . where do you want to sleep?

KARI: On the water bed.

BOB: Okay, go ahead, we're still at the party.

KARI: (Leaves, but returns to room full of adults) Bobi?

BOB: Yes, Kari.

KARI: You know why I want to sleep in the water bed?

KARI: Cause if I wet the bed it won't matter.

Name_____

Class_____

Test 3. The New Republic: A Struggle for Unity and Democracy

OBJECTIVE QUESTIONS

_____ 1. Which of the following events strikingly dramatized the internal weakness of the United States under the Articles of Confederation?
  a. the Whiskey Rebellion
  b. Shays' Rebellion
  c. the Jay Treaty
  d. the War of 1812

__c__ 2. The events of the Confederation period _____ most clearly the weakness of:
  a. the Presidency.
  b. the state governments.
  c. the national congress.
  d. the Supreme Court.

__a__ 3. The Constitution of 1787 differed m_____
  a. the creation of a strong federal
  b. the listing of a bill of rights.
  c. the creation of a national con_____
  d. the granting of taxing power

__c__ 4. The so-called "Great Compromi_____ the Constitution of 1787 led to
  a. the Supreme Court.
  b. the Presidency.
  c. two houses in Congress.
  d. the Bill of Rights.

__a__ 5. A new constitution became _____ 1787 mainly in order to:
  a. strengthen the conce_____
  b. protect the rights an_____
  c. carry out the princi_____
  d. grant the states the_____

__b__ 6. Those delegates who _____ supported the creatio_____
  a. political parties.
  b. the electoral co_____
  c. the Bill of Rig_____
  d. none of the a_____

__c__ 7. Which of the fol_____ non-slave states
  a. the comme_____
  b. the elastic_____
  c. the three_____
  d. the supr_____

__d__ 8. The comme_____
  a. states_____
  b. fugiti_____
  c. coun_____
  d. state_____

Society in general is highly prejudiced toward efficiency and efficiency is a highly rational concept.

The prejudice toward ratcon is reflected in all texts, curriculum guides, and political speeches that dominate the scene.

Strangely enough, the compulsion toward the ratcon side of the diagrams is also easily described as a neurosis. Rational neurosis is a compulsion toward proof, accuracy, authenticity, and conformity to procedures. Although these qualities can be respected and used by many creative people, the compulsion toward them is a neurotic manifestation of rationality. Thus, neurosis as an inhibiting influence to precon processes and creativity is identifiable in *both uncon and ratcon processes.*

Copyright © 1971 by Addison-Wesl

49

THE MEADOW IS RIPE,
THE HARVEST IS SOON.
FENCES CAN KEEP ME OUT
AND A SUDDEN UNEXPECTED STORM
CAN WHIP THE GRASS TO RUBBLE.

The quiet yet effective method of acceptance makes the precon processes legitimate. No analysis is needed for me to cherish the sky or indulge in the odor of a flower. A human is unique and does not belong to a rationally descriptive prescription. So too are the workings of his mind. The smell of the candles of your first birthday cake are residing in your preconscious.

I once saw a child stuff her hand into a glass of milk and thrust the contents over the edge. She reveled in brand new discovery—the genius of Archimedes—but she did it in a way that could give birth on some distant day to an idea. Her mother was accepting because she helped the child draw pictures on the tabletop with the spilled milk.

Creativity requires a kind of mental and emotional freedom that comes only in environments of openness and acceptance. Creative people are usually the survivors of environments of judgment and rational conscious dominance. Humans growing up in such environments often have value-prejudices that are in conflict with where they want to be. This makes the survivors reasonably strong rebels.

Personality postures, value-prejudices, and now preconscious processes . . . the bricks, the mortar, and the space not used. These are constructs against which each of us can judge ourselves. Now to move toward actualization as a concept.

caring sometimes hurts...
but never as much
as the alternative...
not caring

self-actualization

Just as the preconscious is the meadowland of creativity, each human being is a potential orchestra. In life it is too easy to achieve the mastery of only one or two of the parts of what each of us could be. Partly, this is the result of calling into play only a portion of what we are. With the total person being filtered by core-personality characteristics, experiential backgrounds, and tacit or real external pressures, it is miraculous that the concept of self-actualization ever became a reality. The concept is in itself difficult to verbalize for there are far too many extrinsic pressures focused on denying the intrinsic qualities of the individual. Under the easily recognized coercions "to belong . . . to fit . . . to be a success . . . to make a contribution," humans often get caught up in the vise of today's compulsion toward technocratic efficiency or in yesterday's limiting ethical categories. Because we as humans spend much time observing, describing, and interpreting the world around us, we often become conceptual wardens of a prison of perception. My experience and the value-prejudices born of them strongly influence the message of this book. Objectivity, a relative concept at best, is largely missing from these pages. However, the categories I have chosen to communicate these ideas are all expandable and the relationships are all chosen to free or liberate rather than confine.

Actualization is a blend of all we are . . . with a strong vector or thrust toward a positive realization of a higher state of goodness. Actualization is a movement toward the good. It is better achieved when the incredible reservoir of the preconscious is acknowledged and all of the informal, intuitive, tacit knowings of all our experience are brought to bear. Actualization is more a verb than a noun. It must be *done* and not merely intellectualized about. Learning to love requires more than reading Rod McKuen, and actualization requires more than reading Abraham Maslow.

I CAN BE A CHILD—
A FEMALE OR MALE.
I CAN BE BLACK
OR BROWN OR ANY COLORED.
I CAN BE EDUCATED
OR NOT.
NOTHING CAN PREVENT ME FROM

reaching

MAN'S REACH SHOULD EXCEED HIS GRASP.

—ANONYMOUS

well—maybe sometimes

CAPACITY ACTION ASPIRATION

CAPACITY is what I am capable of enduring
ACTION is what I do
ASPIRATION is what I hope to do

Self-actualization comes from bringing these three characteristics of humanness to fruition. The closer they are to equilibrium the closer the individual is to actualization. Many humans have specialized foci on these categories in that one or the other is out of balance with the others. When capacity dominates a strange kind of passivity prevails. The human endures and endures and nothing happens. If action is dominant there is an unfulfilled kind of frustration that comes from doing a job well with the kind of stagnation that comes from perfection setting in early. With aspiration only, there is a Candide-like hopeful optimism that dreams itself into oblivion with high focus on what could be, but no capacity or action to achieve growth.

I LOVE
the THINGS I DO
BECAUSE I AM BEGINNING TO BE SU
THAT THEY ARE
IMPORTAN

I am GLA
SO VERY GLA
THAT I CAN DO
THESE THINGS

Self-actualization in psychological thinking comes from a shift from the man-as-animal characteristics of Freudian approaches and the man-as-an-object characteristics of scientific behaviorism. This extension of concept is rooted in the courage shown by Abraham Maslow in vigorously modifying the historical premises of psychology. Freud rose to fame championing the characteristics of humans viewed as animals with the innate characteristics of beast always present in the unconscious. Later, humans were cast from Darwinian animalistic beginnings into the role of objects by scientists prejudiced toward objective scientific study. Objectivity was the religion and measurement the technique. Humans then became objects, little more than rats in mazes, integers in equations, or categories to be manipulated. Humans became the psychologists' counterpart of the geologists' rocks, the astronomers' stars, and the physicists' subatomic particles. The people watchers took over.

As soon as two human beings relate in detachment as observer to observed, as soon as the observer claims to be aware of nothing more than the behavioral surface of the observed, an invidious hierarchy is established which reduces the observed to a lower status. Of necessity he falls into the same category with all the stupid things of the world that fill Out-There. For consider the gross impertinence of this act of detached observation. Psychologist confronting his laboratory subject, anthropologist confronting tribal group, political scientist confronting voting public . . . in all such cases what the observer may very well be saying to the observed is the same: "I can perceive no more than your behavioral facade. I can grant you no more reality or psychic coherence than this perception allows. I shall observe this behavior of yours and record it. I shall not enter into your life, your task, your condition of existence. Do not turn to me or appeal to me or ask me to become involved with you. I am here only as a temporary observer whose role is to stand back and record and later to make my own sense of what you seem to be doing or intending. I assume that I can adequately understand what you are doing or intending without entering wholly into your life. I am not particularly interested in what *you* uniquely are; I am interested only in the general pattern to which you conform. I assume I have the right to use you to perform this process of classification. I assume I have the right to reduce all that you are to an integer in my science."

T. Roczak, *The Making of the Counter Culture*, New York: Doubleday, 1969, p. 222.

IN THE VERY ACT OF AS
DITION AND DEVELOPIN
SCRIPTION, TWO GENER
DENIED IN THEIR EVALU
CHARACTERISTICS OF H
COMPASSION .. COMMU

The psychology of actualization includes a major emphasis on the role of will. Humans possess will to a degree unseen in laboratory animals. They genetically carry the capacity to care, to communicate, and to dedicate themselves to commitments of their choosing. A key to the concept of actualization is a recognition of the role of will. Environmental constraints can be interpreted as holding you back or helping you grow. Actualization starts when the negative qualities of one's experience are perceived of as having growth potential. The will to use the reality of our lives as steps toward healthy actualization is within each of us. This growth kind of will, if allowed, can counteract the will to be ensnared and constrained by a negative view of reality.

ING THE HUMAN CON-
HE PATTERNS FOR PRE-
ONS OF PSYCHOLOGISTS
ONS THE FUNDAMENTAL
AN BEINGS . . . . .
ATION . . COMMITMENT

Does it make any difference which side of the coin you study? . . . heads or tails? Most psychologists have been concerned with studying people whose behavior has been assessed as *sick*! What would it be like to develop an attitude toward human potential based on *healthy, happy humans* as opposed to those crippled by the vicious handicaps of mental illness?

CORRECTIVE MEDICINE DIFFERS FROM PREVENTATIVE. IS YOUR ATTITUDE TOWARD THE HUMAN CONDITION PREJUDICED TOWARD PREVENTATIVE OR CORRECTIVE?

attitude toward the role of the human in psychology.
language styles is as real as a prejudice against an
structural prejudice contained in the alphabet and
to simply start reading at the bottom of a page. The
training and experience lies a procedural resistance
proach new solutions. However, inside your
resides both a resistance and a compulsion to ap-
paragraph is written. Inside your intrinsic style
insight into it, check yourself out on the way this
approach the solution of a problem or develop your
If you do not think your training affects the way you

Which of the following are most important in life? (Choose one.)

26. Hobbies are:
    a) unimportant
    b) enjoyable
    c) ways to avoid reality
    d) liberating diversions

27. Professional-personal involvement should be:
    a) clearly defined
    b) expected by superiors
    c) as deemed by individuals
    d) discreet

28. Children need education to
    a) provide them with mechanisms to avoid the mistakes of the past
    b) prepare them to understand themselves
    c) avoid the problems of the future
    d) invent what they uniquely are as humans

If you understand the difference between corrective and prescriptive, your answers will show you the way to write the next ten items of this imaginary test.

Acceptance is the most singular characteristic of self-actualization. Although acceptance does not always mean agreement, it is always the first step. Accepting is a wholly different act than rejection. By engaging in it the human begins to learn as much from nonproductive experience as from productive. Each element of involvement becomes an access route to growing insights and exploration.

FAILURE IS POSITIVE FEEDBACK FAILURE IS POSITIVE FEEDBACK FAILURE

Though failure is not sought after by an actualizing human it is not considered to be as bad as we are taught by our extrinsic culture to think it is. External criteria for performance always gives us an outside-looking-in view of failure and success for each individual. For the actualizing person, failure and success are far more intrinsic. That is, they are considered in terms of having provided useful information, experience, and achievement on the basis of internal goal orientation as opposed to external goal orientation.

MOTIVATION

SAFETY ⟷ GROWTH

AUTHORITARIAN   DEPENDENCY   INTRINSIC   TRANS-INTRINSIC   PAN-INTRINSIC

The real issue in actualization is the nature of motivation. Safety motivated people are controlled by the "outside," thus fall easily into the authoritarian and dependency categories. They focus on externals, they see the "outside" as a dangerous and frightening place, they maintain their "inside" as the only place it's safe. They welcome you and try to coerce you into their safety networks, which in turn increases their safety. They tend to feel that if you don't believe, then something bad will happen to you.

Growth motivation takes a person even beyond the level of the intrinsic. A trans-intrinsic person can be anyone—a teacher, a parent, an office manager. It's a person who seeks growth and invites all those around to grow as well. However, trans-intrinsic people never say which brand of growth others should pursue. So it is with the pan-intrinsic, the Buckminster Fuller—Jonas Salk type person who starts from the intrinsic, then grows to confront global problems in a meaningful way.

Critics of the concepts of actualization focus on the image of intrinsic humans as being selfish. Hardly. The person trending toward actualization does not exhibit selfishness nor selflessness, but rather selfness. Here's how it works.

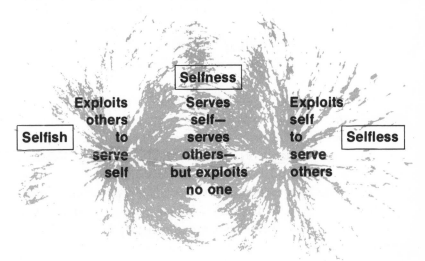

Actualization is a life role in which the capacities, actions, and potentials described on page 57 come to fullest flower. Most actualized people are probably not famous. Instead they cook well, love well, and enjoy life to the fullest. If they cannot go to San Francisco or Paris, they celebrate their houseplants or go to a vacant lot. Their energy is spent on growth. Guilt, anguish, and agony never consume them, even though they occasionally feel these emotions. They are humans deeply in touch with their life energy and they invest it well. When it is important to write ten thousand words or paint a house, they do so. When it is important to take a warm bath or watch a bird, they do so.

AMERICAN TO A BALINESE DANCER: What other forms of art do you have in Bali?

DANCER (smiles): Oh, we have not art in Bali . . . we do everything as well as possible.

67

In an actualizing person the total human is dealt with. There are no priorities shown between intellectuality, emotionality, and sexuality. Society and the human experiences generally associated with it often provide priorities that deny emotionality and sexuality. In most human backgrounds the repression of these two qualities represents a deficit in development. The result is that tendencies that reinstate or legitimize their acknowledgement often are overemphasized.

In the case of emotionality, this reinstatement is manifested in the recent explosion of interest in encounter groups and approaches that legitimize emotional expression. A weakness in encounter is that it often results in competitive expression of emotionality and does not nurture a legitimacy of emotional living, but rather it nurtures a survival of emotional catharsis. In the case of sexuality, social repression often when removed results in a frantic surge to make up for all the time that's been wasted.

Overindulgence is in a strong sense a safety motivation technique. The frantic surge toward emotionality and sexuality is often a motivation *away* from repression rather than toward growth. To know the difference we cannot judge behavior alone. Motivation is the key.

In the next two chapters we will explore motivation within the context of self. Once a human understands his own motivation and then accepts the responsibility of will, then actualization can begin and grow. That's what the next two chapters are about. We've covered all the lectures, now the laboratory is about to begin.

5

(insight)

the actualizing environment

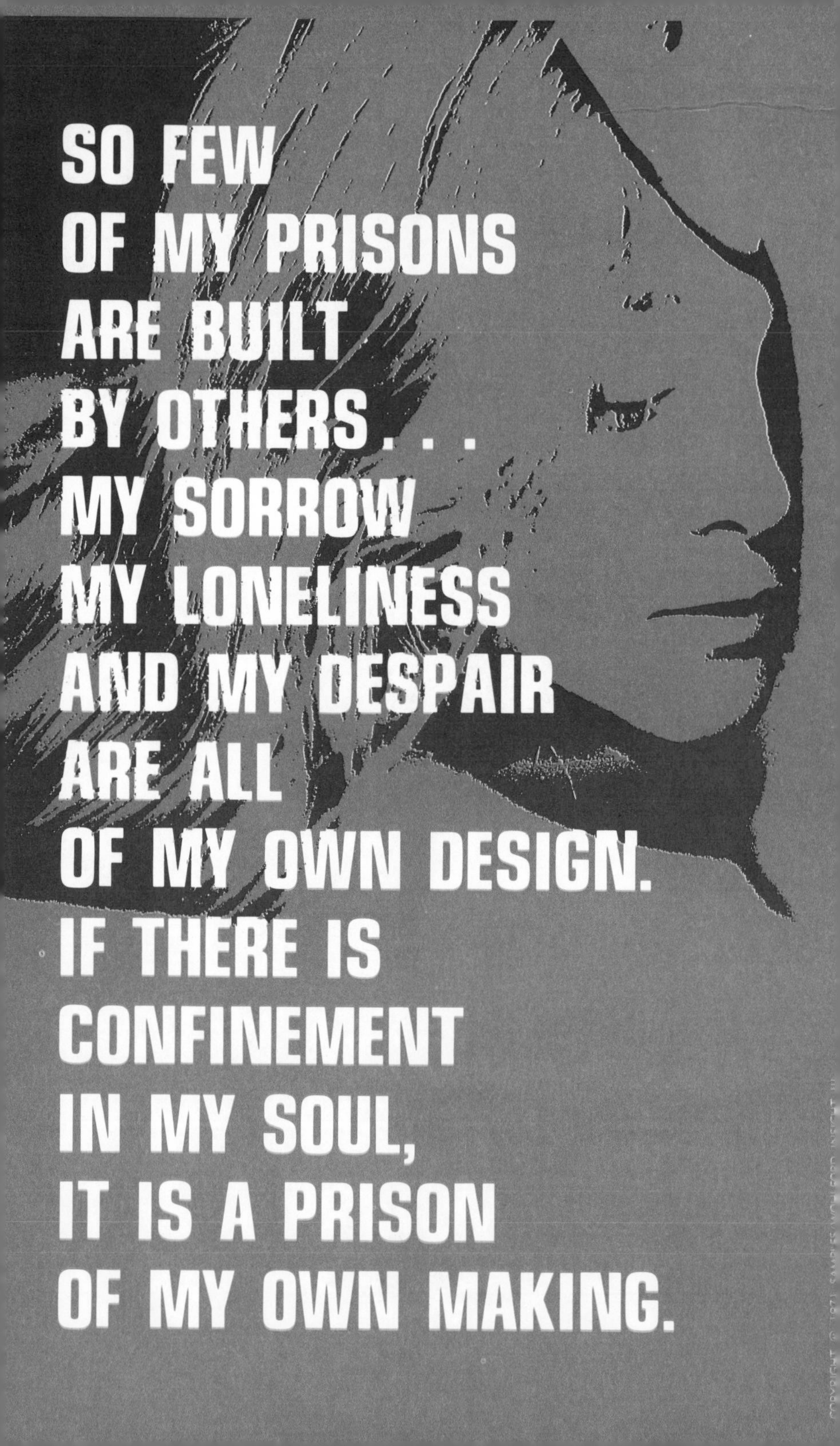

SO FEW
OF MY PRISONS
ARE BUILT
BY OTHERS . . .
MY SORROW
MY LONELINESS
AND MY DESPAIR
ARE ALL
OF MY OWN DESIGN.
IF THERE IS
CONFINEMENT
IN MY SOUL,
IT IS A PRISON
OF MY OWN MAKING.

As should be obvious by now each individual is an environment. This intimate environment contains the value-prejudices, the fears, the love, the courage, and all of those qualities that hang about in our inner museum to affect the way we indulge in the world. This is the first environment that must be known if progress toward actualization is to become a reality.

Unlike *en*counter approaches this approach will focus on *in*counter.

Encounter requires the presence of others and a willingness on your part to share your intimate environment with them. It is a fine approach if there is a compassionate and talented leader. The inner selves of the group can be exposed and shared, and the individuals can grow under the leadership of such a person. However, there are two characteristics that I consider to be counter to actualizing approaches if mismanaged.

First, encounter is a dependency posture. There is a tacit assumption that you can't do this job by yourself.

Second, encounter often becomes emotionally competitive. Participants in encounter do not usually have the time to indulge in the intimacy of their own ego before having to cope with others. This nurtures competition if an attitude of acceptance has not first been established.

SO . . . .

DO YOUR

Incounter starts with IN. So this means you must get inside yourself. Find out what your personality's intrinsic instincts are. You probably have lots of cues already after having read this far. But *in*counter requires more . . . it is a technique done in the silence of self that sensitizes you to yourself.

In talking earlier about capacities, actions, and aspirations we said that bringing these to equilibrium constituted our view of actualization and entry into the being, actualizing state.

The instincts toward being are as real in each of us as are the instincts to basic needs. However they are most easily deferred. The emphasis many developmental psychologists, sociologists, and educators place on food, shelter, etc., is not applicable to the bulk of contemporary society. Where there is a deprivation of these basic needs, actualization is nearly impossible.

Actualization is related to needs such as truth, goodness, beauty, wholeness, aliveness, uniqueness, simplicity, totality, etc. The list is much longer, but innate in the intrinsic capacity of each of us is the capacity to bring such need-values to fruition. Nothing that follows is magic; it will just help you know where some of your filters to actualization are.

ACCEPT
DON'T
EVALUATE

ACCEPTANCE IS A MANDATE . . . REMEMBER THAT ACCEPTANCE DOES NOT NECESSARILY MEAN AGREEMENT. RIGHT NOW YOU ARE WHAT YOU ARE. LATER YOU CAN WORRY ABOUT WHAT YOU WANT TO BE. YOUR CAPACITIES HAVE SO FAR BEEN FULFILLED BY WHAT IT IS THAT YOU ARE, YOUR ACTIONS AND ASPIRATIONS ARE YET TO COME. LEARN TO SENSE YOUR TRUE RESPONSE IN THE SUBTLE, SUPPOSEDLY NON-THREATENING COMFORT OF YOUR HOME, CLASSROOM, CAR, AND EVEN BATHROOM. YOU ARE THE COMMON DENOMINATOR OF YOUR ENTIRE WORLD.

AN ACTUALIZING PHYSICIST MIGHT WORK SOME OF THESE PROCEDURES OUT THIS WAY.

first order equations to achieve actualization

(A)

assumed prior condition equation

$$YOU + EXTRINSIC\ ORDER (EO) = DEFICIENCY\ ORIENTATION$$

$\therefore$ ZERO ACTUALIZING POTENTIAL

assume EXTRINSIC ORDER (EO) to diminish so that

$$YOU + EXTRINSIC\ ENTROPY (EE) = GROWTH\ ORIENTATION$$

$\therefore$ Actualizing potential can approach ∞

> *Note this is because it puts you in the role of an inventor of order. Ordinarily you are an inheritor of order.

check condition

$$YOU + ENTROPY = \infty A$$

~~therefore~~ $\therefore^{?}$ (let's stay scientific)

INCREASE ENTROPY in your world then invent a new order born of your new awareness of yourself.

PROCEDURE : Disrupt routines and order in your own personal day-to-day life style (careful about involving others — this is your personal trip — NOT theirs.

TRY GOING FROM ENTROPY TO EMPATHY BY FINDING OUT ABOUT YOURSELF AND THEN INVENTING THE NEW ORDER YOU WANT.

Your reaction to the increased entropy in your environment is real. Chances are the order you have established came from an imposed or inherited ethic. Kind of a "a place for everything and everything in its place" ethic.

But by breaking up your order *you* have two actualizing qualities that can extend your action and aspiration base in the direction of growth instead of safety. These are:

1) The environment is now "structured" to allow you to invent the order *you* believe in.
and
2) The environment is structured to let you know about the triviality (or maturity) of your attitudes of acceptance.

TRY THESE:

- **How do you feel when you abandon habits when trying to find a tablespoon?**
- How does spaghetti and red wine make you feel at breakfast?
- Do you like some forks better than others?
- Do other coffee mugs work as well as the one you usually choose?
- Have you standardized your hair style to avoid changing your appearance?
- Do you get annoyed when you are trying to find matching shoes in your closet?
- Do you intend to restore order as it was?
- How much do the value-prejudices you have about these things orient you toward growth or toward safety?
- DO THESE THINGS . . . DON'T JUST READ THEM!

DO IT YOURSELF ENTROPY KIT

BEFORE

AFTER

BEFORE

AFTER

BEFORE

AFTER

The questions on page 77 are of the short-answer variety. None are seeking justification . . . only information. The nature of core personality and acceptance is real. Each possesses within it a tendency to defer or to accept. Authoritarian and dependency cores are responsibility-deferring postures. The intrinsic core personality is a responsibility-accepting posture.

Now that you have some guidelines to play with entropy and your reaction to it, try engaging yourself with others. But keep quiet about what you find out. This is *IN*counter, remember.

CHECK THE SOURCE OF EACH EMOTION YOU FEEL

is it inside you— or outside?

Teacher: O.K. gang, pay attention because this assignment will last the rest of the week.

(Teacher turns to chalkboard begins to write, chalk breaks and class giggles. Teacher whirls around angrily)

Teacher :   All right, I said *pay attention*!

Lover I: Nobody could make me feel as good as you do.

Lover II: No it's you that makes me feel good.

Lover I: But you couldn't feel as good as I do.

Parent: You know it makes grandma feel better when you kiss her.

Child: But mother, I'm eighteen, how do you think she makes *me* feel when I kiss her.

Hard Hat: To think you presume to live in the same world as me disgusts me.

Hippie: Look man, your world is the reason I live as I do. *You* disgust me!

No one else can make you feel anything. Your anger, your love, your expression of fear is a world of your own making. Each time you externalize the source of an emotion you are flashing a signal to yourself of responsibility for deference.

The teacher feared losing control. He assumed he held control, but *they* had control.

The lovers were busy making each other responsible for the good they felt. Soon they would try externalizing *bad* feelings as well.

The parent exemplified an ethic that she assigned to grandmother. The teenager assigned his feelings to grandmother.

The hard hat blames his fear, shown by disgust, on the hippie. The hippie gets his ethic by playing off the hard hat.

The great emotional giveaway testifies to external fate control. Actualization requires internal fate control.

STOP ASKING OTHER PEOPL
WHY QUESTIONS

WHEN YOU ASK ANOTHER HUMAN BEING "WHY" YOU ARE ASKING HIM TO *JUSTIFY* AN ACT, ATTITUDE, OR RELATIONSHIP. *WHY* IS THE MOST THREATENING QUESTION THAT CAN BE ASKED!

"Why do you love me?"
"Why don't you love me?"

"Why did you vote for that bastard?"

"Why is it that everytime I come home you have to tell me about Linda?"

"Why, why, why. Why do you always ask why?"
"Why shouldn't I?"

When you ask another human being "Why," he should be paying you fifty dollars an hour for the privilege. Why is psychoanalytic. It *requires* justification. It forces the answerer into the defensive. It says loudly you have done something wrong (or right). It pre-supposes evaluation. When you ask *why*, you tacitly signal the person you have asked to justify his position.

Why can only be asked when trust levels are incredibly high . . . that is, after you have received permission to ask. A ploy I once used while trying to become a scientist was to say I had the right to ask the universe WHY? I tried it for nearly ten years and *it never answered*.

When you start catching yourself asking why . . . accept the responsibility for non-acceptance. If non-acceptance is a habit with you then you know how you may habitually avoid actualization.

STOP ASKING YOURSELF WHY UNTIL YOU DEAL WITH WHAT YOU FEEL

ONE OF THE SUREST FORMS OF AVOIDANCE IS THE SELF QUESTION "WHY". IT IS AN INVITATION TO AN INTELLECTUAL EXCURSION THAT RATIONALIZES FEELINGS INTO THE BACKGROUND. INCOUNTER IS FIRST AN INCURSION INTO "WHAT".

"Why did I vote for him?"

"Why did I get so angry at her?"

"Why did I let myself get so upset at that principal?"

"Why is it that I like pizza better with beer?"

"Why do I get tense around Christmas?"

Actualization, though innate, is easily avoided. One sure mechanism is to analyze too soon. *Why* is the clincher question of western man. Its pursuit has led us into the electronic, machine dominated society that we currently have. It is taught to children as being the most important question in that in childhood it is inevitably linked to stress. "Why are you making so much noise when your daddy is tired?" . . . or . . . "My God, Linda, why did you have to drop a *full* jar of paint?"

Rationality has *why* as its watchword, but using premature rationality to seek safety is an indicator that we fear the condition or problem that forces us to ask it. *Why* is usually a device to move toward safety whether asking it of others or ,yourself. Use *why*, both the intrinsic and extrinsic *why*, as a clue that you are moving *toward safety and not growth*. Once you are aware of this safety motivation, you can then determine what is causing it.

SPEAK IN THE FIRS
IN THE DECLARATIV

A LINGUISTIC HABIT ROOTED IN COURTEOUS SPEECH IS ALSO RESPONSIBLE FOR TACIT AVOIDANCE. SAYING "WE" OR "YOU" WHEN "I" IS MEANT IS AN ACT THAT INCLUDES OTHERS IN MY CONCLUSIONS AND STATEMENTS, USUALLY WITHOUT THEIR PERMISSION.

Asking *why* of others is a hassle to them, but in many ways so is *every* question. If I build a tendency to use each question I ask as a signal that sensitizes me toward a realization that I am putting someone on the defensive, I can become aware of how habitually I do it.

Someone once said it was never the great big problems that destroyed love affairs, but the little annoyances that killed them. Always asking people questions constitutes one of these annoyances and so too does speaking in the second and third person to include others in my decisions.

Questions and second-third person references and inclusions erode trust and connote a lack of acceptance.

PERSON AND ONLY TO OTHER PEOPLE

WE JUST LOVE TO SHOP—DON'T WE, *DEAR?*

Such habitual speaking patterns tell much about one's attitudes toward deference. People who have tried this step of the INcounter approach have said it was one of the most powerful of the incounter steps—*primarily because it was so subtle.*

ACCEPT *DON'T* EVALUATE . . . !

Tourist: (Horseback with Navaho) "Wow, isn't this a beautiful canyon."

Navaho: (Snickering)

Tourist: (Rides in silence)

Tourist: "What a beautiful stream."

Navaho: (Laugh)

Tourist: "Why are you laughing?"

Navaho: "A river is a river, a canyon is a canyon. Do not make them over with your words. Accept them for what they are."

This anecdote surprised us when we first heard it in that it made us even more aware of how tacitly we are compelled to evaluate. Evaluation appears to be a virtue and those who evaluate best are by far and away the most virtuous. That is no more or less a part of the neurosis of a competitive western technocracy. We build school systems, political systems, and in a subtle way emotional systems, on evaluative premises.

Lovers often ask for or give comparisons on everything from cooking to sexual performance. They count anniversaries, gifts, telephone calls, the number of days since they last did something. It becomes more important that "This is the *best* backrub you've ever given me" than that "I enjoy having my back rubbed!"

Evaluative comments are almost always tacitly comparative and are often subtle ways of trying to control others' behavior to create conditions of safety. This is distinctly in opposition to growth-motivated postures. Counting is the real payoff. I knew a man who counted each girl friend he had. He role played the "cool" actualized person because it gave him a manipulative advantage in certain circles. He would often say such endearing things as "I've been with three hundred and twelve girls and you are the greatest." He *says* his success is related to his self-actualization, yet he somehow can't realize why girls choose not to invest much of importance in him.

Remember, as a posture, acceptance is not agreement. So don't get lost in the semantic quagmire that says "this is all bull because it means I have to accept Charles Manson and other psychopathic murders." There is little your acceptance or agreement can do about murder and murderers. You cannot wish them away anymore than we can scare away the Vietnams or Biafras by wearing bell bottom pants. *I must accept but not agree with such entities.* I may also accept the responsibility to *do* something rather than talk and evaluate.

About ten pages ago you encountered *in*counter. Some people with whom we have worked have been exposed exactly as you have. They told us about their experience in a variety of ways. Some were coworkers, some teachers, some students. Some met at conventions, some were lovers, and some were completely distant in towns we had never visited.

*In*counter works. It works as much as you choose to let it. Some who have been teachers gave the rules to their students and made it into an encounter situation. Some did it quietly at home and at work.

Some said they played at first as though it was some silly game. They mussed up the silverware drawer and then fussed as they looked for an olive fork and *then* . . .
they realized. *The olive fork owned them rather than their owning it.*

The petty annoyances they felt as they played incounter gave them a new awareness about themselves. Even when they extended it into the lives and presence of others they had enough awareness and sensitivity *not* to fear growth. They said they grew.

You are beautiful because
like a flower
you are growing.
You love the sun and rain.
You bend and bow in the wind.
You catch the last snowflakes
of winter
and fill the gray sky
with your light.
Through all the seasons
of my life
I will love the times
we grew and bloomed together.

GROW

WE
NEVER
SOLVE
PROBLEMS
WE
JUST
GET
TIRED
OF
THEM

GROWTH WANTS SUNLIGHT
GROWTH WANTS WATER
GROWTH WANTS NUTRIENTS
GROWTH WANTS CARE

Here are some more:

STOP SCAPEGOATING—

Whenever you blame anyone for anything, you are scapegoating. It is the first act of exhibiting prejudice.
"I could feel better about loving you if I hadn't been raised a Catholic."

CHECK COMPETITIVE IMPULSES—

Competition is seldom internal. It is a compulsion toward which we have been conditioned by extrinsic society. It is one of the most unnatural of human activities. Each time competitive impulses arise recognize this as an extrinsic focus.
"I want a Porsche just to see the expression on her face."

START A JOURNAL—

My most useful game was incountering myself in a very private but very honest journal. As I looked back on a year of my life while I was threshing about in a comical *and* deeply moving love affair, I found facets of my badly cut jewel that really needed polishing. Mostly my dishonesty became obvious.

I can't lie to me but I could lie to others. When I found I had done so I realized I wrote the journal to *her* and not to me.

Some excerpts follow . . . Try one yourself.

When I chose to feel love and express
it to her I was bewildered by her
resentment of the act. I sensed her
anxiety and tried to placate her.
STUPID.... I TREATED IT LIKE IT WAS
MY PROBLEM... it wasn't it was

hers

I KNOW NOW THAT SHE INVITES MY LOVE AND
THEN RESENTS MY GIVING IT... SHE IS
A FANTASTIC TEASE... INVITING CLOSENESS
AND THEN REJECTING IT IN FEAR... I
CAN'T CRITICIZE HER BECAUSE IT IS MY
DESIRE TO BE CLOSE. IF I CAN'T, THEN
I HAVE TO GET THE COURAGE TO SAY
GOODBYE.

I WANT TO BE CLOSE.. I HAVE
HAD IT WITH TRIVIAL RELATIONSHIPS

I REALLY WANT
TO BE WITH SOME
-ONE WHO WANTS
TO BE WITH ME
WITHOUT MAKING
ME OVER INTO
SOME FORMULA
LOVER. I WANT
TO BE WITH SOME
- ONE WHO IS
STRONG ENOUGH
WITH THEMSELVES
NOT TO SEARCH
FOR CUES FROM
ME TO DETERMINE
HOW THEY SHOULD
ACT.

I WANT US
EACH TO
BE OUR
SELVES

I want adventures in life. If someone
came to live with me I want to exist
not as a group of two...but two groups
of one... Two people can live
together as individuals. I can only
love an individual... I can never
love a group.

I want myself and the girl to be alive
in the acts ~~of~~ and processes of expl-
oring places that matter. These places
are fields, flowers, movies paintbrushes,
continents, sex, food, bathtubs and...
more —— I want no feeling of obligation
to do these together all the time.

AM WRITING THIS TO CLEAN UP THE PAIN I FEEL
ECAUSE I HAVE NOT COMMUNICATED WITH THE
IRL I LOVE FOR FORTY-FIVE DAYS. NOW AS
TRY ALL I SENSE IS A FRIGHTENED, BITTER
REATURE THAT CANT ACCEPT MY CONCERN
ND SHOWS IT WITH AN ABSENCE OF COM-
ASSION NOT AT ALL LIKE HER ——

WE NEVER SOLVE PROBLEMS; WE JUST GET TIRED OF THEM

IF YOU ARE TIRED OF *NOT* GROWING, JUST START GROWING! MANY PEOPLE I KNOW WHO HAVE MOVED TOWARD ACTUALIZATION SAID ALL THEY HAD TO DO TO GET RID OF A DEFICIENCY- OR DEPENDENCY-ORIENTED TRAIT WAS TO FIRST REALLY *BELIEVE* THAT IT WAS INSIDE THEM AND THEN *SIMPLY TURN IT OFF.*

Some said it wasn't that simple . . . they said they had to pay the principal *and* the interest without benefit from the fairness in lending act.

A VALUE ISN'T WORTH A DAMN UNLESS IT IS A VERB

BECOMING
A LEARNER
LEARNER B

DRIVING TOWARD ACTUALIZATION

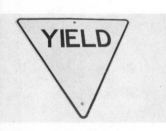

Try driving to work in an accepting fashion
Learn to accept whatever happens as a posi
tive indicator of *your* skill, *your* insight, an
your acceptance. Build a more positive view
of your capacity and potential to learn than t
take offence and reject.

VIEWING TOWARD ACTUALIZATION

TV is a goldmine learning environment an
yet more energy is spent grouching about th
fact that it isn't the BBC, than trying to reall
learn from the medium. The medium *is* th
message and it's full of messages. Turn th
sound off, scramble the picture, but forc
yourself to learn about yourself as you view

A LEARNER BECOMING ECOMING A

COOKING TOWARD ACTUALIZATION

Cook something you do not have a recipe for. Continue until you feel you have it right. Check your feelings out as you progress. Really risk and do this for guests . . . that you have never cooked for.

SHOPPING TOWARD ACTUALIZATION

Go to a supermarket, preferably with children. Check out your pattern of anxieties as the kids explore this incredibly seductive environment. If you don't have or can't borrow kids treat the trip like a visit to a museum. What do you find that is difficult to accept?

Please write something important to yourself on this page.

the actualizing environment (outsight)

Love is not freedom . . .
If I love you
I am using a part of me
that usually belongs only to me.
If I love you
I must be willing to accept that

All of this book so far has been focused on you, on the important qualities of self that tend to inhibit actualization. Maslow argued well that the capacity for actualization is as genetically determined in the human species as the ability to speak. Love is as real in us as writing and conceptualizing.

However, history and society often see things differently. There are large numbers of us . . . we are being forced together . . . and at the same time a new religion that has overtaken us all threatens all the old institutions of human invention. This is the religion of technology. Its ethic is subtle, efficient, and effective. Materialism is rapidly replacing Communism and all the other-ism's combined.

Technology creeped in on little cat feet and created an environment of behaviorism. Behaviorism is the psychology of the technocracy. It is the mental ethic of management. The lifeblood of the technocracy management flows through the veins and arteries of management systems.

With this metaphor for reality becoming reality, our environment conditions us to a behavior that, as seen by the humanists, is fundamentally inadequate. *Man can be more*. These pages have tried to create an awareness of the way the technocratic ethic has sculptured you. Now let's get to how you can nourish intrinsic environments. Those consistent with actualization.

As long as you are in touch with one other person you can extend the self-actualization potential of yourself. Carefully though, if you become a zealot you are going to discover that you aren't actualized. Your job isn't to proselytize the universe and make a thousand more you's. The goal is to *be*. The goal is the being-state. The environment grows when there are more being-states in the presence of the universe.

BEING VALUES

WHOLENESS
PERFECTION
COMPLETION
RICHNESS
ALIVENESS
JUSTICE
UNIQUENESS
PLAYFULNESS
SELF-SUFFICIENCY
BEAUTY
EFFORTLESSNESS
GROWTH
HONESTY
EXPLORATION
NEWNESS

DEFICIENCY VALUES

SPECIFICITY
SAFETY
COMPETITIVENESS
SUPERIORITY
SERIOUSNESS
INTERNAL CONSISTENCY
ORDERLINESS
RESPONSIBILITY
COST-BENEFITS
ECONOMY
DEPENDENCY
RULES
PUNISHMENT
REWARDS
STABILITY
FAMILIARITY

partly after Maslow

HE WANTS TO MARRY ME.
WHAT SHOULD I DO?

LOOK, I DON'T KNOW IF IT'S MISPLACED, BUT I BELIEVE ENOUGH IN YOU FOR YOU TO DECIDE. YOU ARE THE PERSON MOST INVOLVED. YOU ARE JOYFUL AND INTELLIGENT—SO, SEE WHERE YOU CAN GROW MOST. ONLY YOU KNOW WHERE THAT IS. I CAN TALK, BUT IT'S ONLY ME. YOU MUST DECIDE, AND WHAT YOU DECIDE WILL BE WHAT HAPPENS.

FIRST, TAKE ALL THE ALTERNATIVES INTO CONSIDERATION AND TRY TO FIGURE OUT WHICH WILL CAUSE YOU THE LEAST PAIN. HE OBVIOUSLY LOVES YOU & YOU CAN GIVE A LITTLE FOR WHAT HE WILL HAVE TO OFFER IN THE FUTURE. ENGINEERS MAKE A LOT OF MONEY AND STATISTICS SHOW THAT THEY SELDOM GET A DIVORCE ONCE THEY HAVE COMMITTED THEMSELVES.

107

WHICH PIGEON DO YOU THINK IS CLOSER TO ACTUALIZATION?

Try these: Respond in both growth and safety.

SAFETY

GROWTH

1. What should I wear to your boss's party?

2. Should I take a tour trip to Mexico?

3. I can't read this French menu...what should I do?

4. Was the movie as good as the book?

5. Miss Jackson, I just wet my pants!

By now it should be clear that real self-actualization can only take place if the core personality is intrinsic. An actualized person and an intrinsic core personality are not uncommitted, nor nondependent or nonauthoritarian. They may be all of these, but there is no compulsion to force their views and commitments on others. Actualized people deal with their commitments in a personal way. Although they may have deep external understandings of their commitments, they still accept the responsibility for them personally.

The actualized woman can attempt to dominate her children and lover . . . but when questioned she will not seek a hiding place in safety-motivated explanations. She would simply admit it was her idea and resolve her emotional, sexual, and intellectual stress at her own expense.

Hopefully, you can also see that the self-inflicted games we asked you to play earlier were efforts to have you create stress situations. Order vs. time is a technocratic formula for stress. The reason for things being in a specific place is to cut down the time, i.e., energy, involved in retrieval. *Technocracy measures, so its goal is the least time invested for maximum gain.*

Are you concerned about how to invest the minimum time for the maximum gain in loving . . . being a parent . . . your job?

WHAT YOU ARE SPEAKS SO LOUDLY PEOPLE CAN'T HEAR WHAT YOU SAY

ME:	The kids seem to be using the Polaroid cameras without a hitch.
TEACHER:	Wow, I thought they would really break the stuff up. I was surprised they could load them at all.
ME:	It always seems to work if you wait long enough . . .
TEACHER:	JACKIE! Pick up that wrapper you dropped!
ME:	(Nothing)
TEACHER:	Darn kids—no sense of responsibility!
ME:	Does that film wrapper really bother you?
TEACHER:	(Amazed) SURE!
ME:	Then *you* pick it up.

If I externalize my value system with directives that do not involve me, I have zero credibility with those to whom I am exposed. If *I* don't pick up paper I cannot honestly suggest that others should. Double standards are sign posts of phoniness.

If *I* interrupt children, I cannot convince children that they shouldn't interrupt me.

If *I* go to bed with anyone I choose and then tell you you cannot, you can never believe me.

If *I* tell children not to complain about other teachers and I gripe about the administration in the teacher's lounge, then I am a hypocrite.

If *I* get ruffled when a girl asks me to move in with her, I am a chauvinist.

If *I* get hacked off at a driver who goes through a stop sign because *he broke the law*, I am definitely not getting too close to actualizing.

ACCEPTANCE DOES NOT MEAN
AGREEMENT . . . IT MEANS
ACCEPTANCE.

We believe that self-actualization is fully possible when a person has free, trusting, joyful access to preconscious processes. That is, actualization comes about when each human has full access to a life style filled with creativeness. Maslow, in his later writings, said that he was beginning to suspect that creativeness and actualization may well be the same thing. Our informal life and experience is as real if not more so than our formal, structured one. Environments can be created to legitimize the preconscious and the first step is to create an atmosphere of awareness and acceptance. Jerome Bruner once said, "A child never gives a wrong answer, he just answers a different question."

The formalistic qualities of our world are divisive, separatist, atomistic, and full of categories. Categories may help in understanding, but they are too easily passed on. Our introduction of categories such as core personalities, conscious, preconscious, and unconscious, is for you (and us) to better understand the intimate environments related to self. And to extend the concept of self to the role it plays in dealing with other people whose self is as precious as ours. Our categories are as subjective and eclectic as any, but we know that on the path to growth they have helped us and others to know the tacit boundary conditions of human contact.

earth, fire, water, and air were once used to describe the substance of the universe. Today's physical scientists have dozens more. Who is right? Both. Oxygen is stuck with being oxygen, but humans can be almost what they want.

A society of individuals steeped in humanism is not yet with us. But this gives no right to masses to create statistical, behavioristic prescriptions to human existence.

The techniques and categories we have introduced are designed to shed light on a different facet of the human condition as related to each of us. If I have a fuller understanding and acceptance of myself, I will be better able to understand and accept others. Creativeness is personal, and so too is actualization. There are no sexual, racial, or religious constraints on actualization. I can be woman or man, craftsman or teacher, rich or poor, and still achieve higher levels of fulfillment if I know myself better and learn to accept the beauty that lives in human differences.

each with
its own
light . . .

each with
its own
fire . . .

judgment and growth

If an actualizing environment exists, the possibilities for experience are flower-like rather than ladder-like. Life becomes a galaxy of new directions to explore, each the choice of the individual and legitimate in the environment.

In actualization also is the innate assumption that growth will proceed toward the good, the noble, and the higher instincts of the human condition. The baser attitudes and instincts give way readily to higher ones if humans have free choice.

This concept is in contradiction to behavioristic, divisive, safety postures. These divisive, deference approaches have so little faith in the human condition that they must establish criteria and evaluative verifications that control and restrain the directions of growth. The individual is usually judged on conformity rather than growth.

CHECK YOUR BEHAVIORAL OBJECTIVES.

DO THEY TRAP OR LIBERATE?

IS YOUR WORLD FULL OF DISTINCTIONS ABOUT WHAT *CANNOT* BE DONE AS OPPOSED TO WHAT CAN BE TRIED?

DOES *YOUR* BEHAVIOR ALWAYS REFLECT *YOUR* MOTIVATION . . . OR DO YOU KNOW HOW TO FAKE A MOTIVATION WITH BEHAVIOR?

IF YOUR BEHAVIOR IS NOT CONSISTENT WITH YOUR MOTIVATION YOU KNOW YOU DO NOT TRUST.

you cannot
learn to be
what you are
unless you are
free
to follow
your beliefs.
the way
i can keep you
from following your
beliefs
is to say
'i trust you'
when
i am really saying . . .
'you know
what i expect
of you . . .
and
i am sure
you will do it.'

Evaluation as it currently exists in schools and society in general is a technocratic influence. The compulsion to evaluate is a kind of neurosis, particularly linked with Western thinking . . . and more specifically with Western technocratic thinking. Evaluation is little more than the act of checking whether or not one's expectations have been met.

One purpose of the previous six chapters is to indicate that you have far more control over your expectations than others might lead you to believe.

The key to the evaluation process is in the expectations, not the process itself. The causes structure the symptoms, not the symptoms, the causes. If you expect a certain kind of behavior, then you structure the kind of environment that nurtures that behavior.

Divisiveness structures specificity and sameness. Openness structures for divergence and uniqueness.

"My children are threatened by questions. They think they have done something wrong because to them questions are unnatural."

"If one student cannot answer a question, the others in the class will refuse to answer it."

"The premium is on compassion not cognition. It is more important to care about each other enough not to answer and possibly embarrass others than to compete with information."

— a Navajo teacher

When someone says,

HOW CAN YOU TREAT ME THIS WAY AFTER ALL I'VE DONE FOR YOU?

What they really mean is . . .

"WHAT I HAVE DONE WAS TO SET YOU UP TO TREAT ME A CERTAIN WAY . . . *AND YOU DIDN'T!*"

WRITE SOME OBJECTIVES FOR THE FOLLOWING CONDITIONS
THAT ARE BOTH LIBERATING AND CONFINING

LIBERATING   CONFINING

1. The way you keep your room in shape.

2. The way you treat me.

3. This week's menu.

4. ~~The ways you save money~~
4. The reasons you save money

5. How often you should make love.

6. The kind of car you should buy.

125

GO.....GO.....
STATUS QUO

The type of result that arises from competition toward the same goals is easily predictable. People get more or less skillful in doing the same thing.

If such practices had applied to architecture, *all* buildings might look like the United Nations building. Since competitive goals seem to be applied to American automobiles they *are* beginning to look alike.

123-41-1. Short title. This article shall be known and may cited as the "Educational Accountability Act of 1971".

123-41-2. Legislative declaration. (1) The general assembly hereby declares that the purpose of this article is to stitute an accountability program to define and measure qualit education, and thus to help the public schools of Colorado such quality and to expand the life opportunities a the students of this state; further, to provide ards assistance in helping their school patrons value of their school program as comp

The purpose of questioning accountability is not to discredit the legitimacy of the concept but to affirm the domain of its source. No suite of criteria are inherently better than others . . . only the motivations for choosing them differ. Do we subscribe to the ethic and criteria of openness to live by ourselves or to control others? The intrinsic choice and responsibility is actualizing. If choices are made upon extrinsic criteria, then conformity and safety are the motives and are delimiting.

smoke, because the LORD descended upon it in ire: and the smoke thereof ascended as the moke of a furnace, and the whole mount quaked reatly.
19 And when the voice of the trumpet sounded g, and waxed louder and louder, Mō'śēś spake, God answered him by a voice.
And the LORD came down upon mount Sī' on the top of the mount: and the LORD called ēś up to the top of the mount; and Mō'śēś up.
nd the LORD said unto Mō'śēś, Go down, the people, lest they break through unto D to gaze, and many of them perish. d let the priests also, which come near to h, sanctify themselves, lest the LORD upon them.
Mō'śēś said unto t ne up to t

12 Honour thy father
thy God giveth thee.
13 Thou shalt not kill.
14 Thou shalt not commit adultery.
15 Thou shalt not steal.
16 Thou shalt not bear false witness thy neighbour.
17 Thou shalt not covet thy neighbour' thou shalt not covet thy neighbour's wife, manservant, nor his maidservant, nor his his ass, nor any thing that is thy neighbou
18 And all the people saw the thunder the lightnings, and the noise of th the mountain smoking: if, they remo

WE HAVE OFTEN HEARD THAT
SUPERFICIAL KNOWLEDGE IS
BANAL . . .

SCHOLARS SAID THIS

WE HAVE OFTEN HEARD THAT
SUPERFICIAL CITIZENS WERE
BANAL . . .

POLITICIANS SAID THIS

WE HAVE OFTEN HEARD THAT
THE UNSOPHISTICATED WERE
BANAL . . .

SOPHISTICATES SAID THIS

WHAT DID THE HUMANS SAY?

Write it on top of the next page

Since most professional journals in the field are suspicious of articles that do not contain at least some statistical material, this tendency is further strengthened. And so eager young sociologists stranded somewhere in hinterland institutions, yearning for the richer pastures of the better universities, supply us with a steady stream of little statistical studies of the dating habits of their students, the political opinions of the surrounding natives or the class system of some hamlet within commuting distance of their campus. It might be added here that this system is not quite so terrible as it may seem to the newcomer to the field, since its ritual requirements are well known to all concerned. As a result, the sensible person reads the sociological journals mainly for the book reviews and the obituaries, and goes to sociological meetings only if he is looking for a job or has other intrigues to carry on.

Quote from *Invitation to Sociology, A Humanistic Perspective* by Peter L. Berger, Anchor Books, 1963, p. 10.

I am capable
of accepting...
of enjoying
and celebrating
the differences
in human beings.

I can love
the blackness of skin
the blueness of eyes
and the fragile smile
given by a child
when he doesn't know
what to do

I can show fear
kindness
honesty and care

I am a whole universe
and
I live in the beautiful
presence of yours.

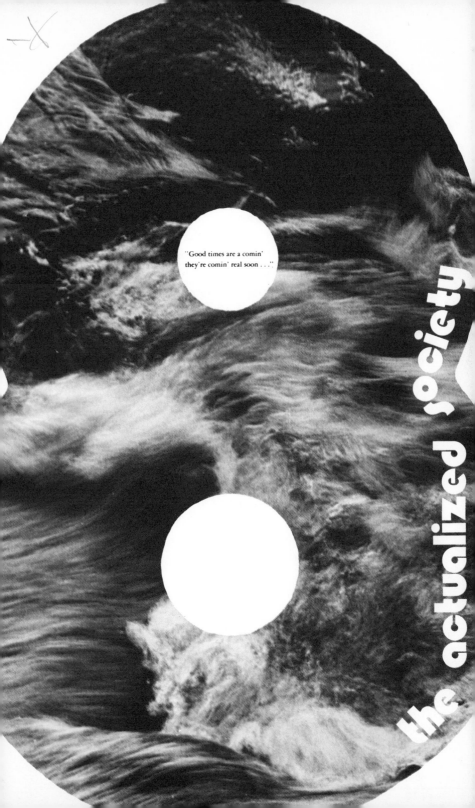

"Good times are a comin'
they're comin' real soon . . ."

the actualized society

The core personality postures of Chapters 1 and 2 . . . the value categories on pages 24, 25 . . . all relate to very definite trends of change in contemporary American society. Though it is true similar changes are taking place in technocratic societies the world over, the critic François Revel, in his book *Without Marx or Jesus,* describes the overwhelming revolution he sees taking place in the fabric of American society.

It is not an event we can wait for, in that it is here and it is happening now. Institutions are changing and this final chapter will be devoted to relating those qualities characteristic of the intrinsic in individuals to two larger schemes. The first will be an account of the changes in schools and the second a consideration of Charles Reich's theses about the evolution of American society.

We believe society is changing in America because individuals are changing. In the same subtle way that biological evolution takes place—as the individuals change, so too does the species. In most biological evolution it is the environment that induces these changes, but with humans it is a different ball game. They control the environment.

This is not the place nor is it our intent to enter the arena of human survival ecology. Instead we will focus on the attitudinal environments that tend to nurture movement toward either safety or growth.

In a way, the fantasy metaphor might be like this . . .

At one time reptiles ruled the earth. While they did what it was that reptiles do best, there lurked in the shadows a little group of creatures some of which watched the dinosaurs do their thing. Which was to *lay eggs.* The littler creatures realized that the dinosaurs went away from their eggs as soon as they were laid . . . and so they creeped in, ate the eggs and grinned at each other. From the standpoint of the dinosaurs, these little creatures were polluting the environment. Their increase couldn't be coped with. But it was effective as there are very few dinosaurs around now.

An authoritarian core personality dinosaur would say

MAMMALS ARE IMMORAL . . . ACCORDING TO THE FIRST COMMANDMENT!

A dependency core personality dinosaur would form a committee and say

HMM! WE'VE GOT TO GET ORGANIZED AND PUT A STOP TO THIS!

An intrinsic core personality dinosaur would say

I'VE GOT TO HIDE MY EGGS BETTER!

UNFORTUNATELY . . . THEY DIDN'T HAVE THE OPTIONS! WE DO!

AUTHORITARIAN

Loving in authoritarian settings is clear-cut. The male dominates and the female submits. Obedience and righteousness prevail. External ethnics describe the propriety of the relationship. If I am male and you question my role, I quote the Bible or any other appropriate source and you get back in line.

DEPENDENCY

Loving in dependency is more like guerrilla warfare than the slave-master schemes of authoritarian loving. There is constant negotiation and coercion. The male still has the tradition in his favor according to the cultural setting. But in dependency, the roles shift. The male uses the institutions of love or marriage or parenting to enhance his own posture and to protect his traditional dominant role. The female tries to attain as much advantage as possible in the face of the long history of being oppressed by these social institutions. This advantage can be in possessions, emotional obedience, motherhood, or alimony.

INTRINSIC

Intrinsic loving has no precedent in terms of historical or social contexts. As a result, the humans involved in it love deeply regardless of their roles. Discourse is related to communication rather than coercion. The male no more relies on past precedents to dominate than the female does to submit. The roles of lovers, parents, or marriage partners are described by commitment to self in each other's presence. Intrinsic lovers know that before you can love someone else, you must love yourself. They create human ecologies where these concepts can flourish.

134

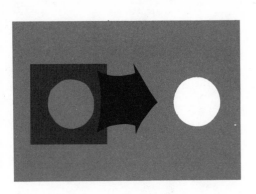

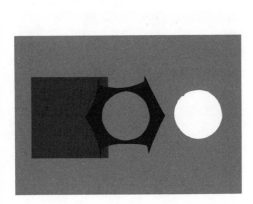

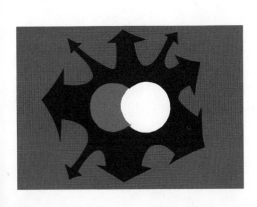

These relationships most certainly reflect the social setting in which life is lived. As the cultural setting evolves and changes, so too does the ecology in which the individual can develop personalities consistent with the culture. However, it is a cop-out posture to believe that the outside must change before the inside can follow. The dinosaurs on the previous pages were prisoners of their genetic capacity. We as humans possess a universe of options that dinosaurs could never imagine. We can become the *instruments* of change in the ecology instead of the *objects* of change. Just as these brief examples of sex roles differ, so too do relationships between parents and children, between ethnic groups, and between nations. Love is a metaphor for life. These three postures relate to the life of the individual, to pairing and family posture, and to the whole of humankind.

What would an intrinsic society be like? Would everyone be selfishly doing their own thing and exploiting every other human being? Would people stop loving, stop caring, stop helping? Would the *kind* be lost from human*kind?*

No! . . . but such concerns are raised often by those who feel the winds of growth blowing across their lives. There is always a little fear in the unknown. But the fear is also exciting. Basic to the philosophy of actualization is a profoundly positive view of humankind. History is replete with examples of people who, in the face of fear, ran screaming into the useless caverns of yesterday. They so feared the shadows on the walls they never sought the sources of light.

If society became actualized and if its inhabitants became intrinsic, little would seem different at first. But then we would begin to notice that the grocer *wanted* to be a grocer, your lover *wanted* to be a lover, and your surgeon *wanted* to be a surgeon. There would no longer be people hiding in roles because they didn't realize they could make choices. The rings of freedom would widen.

the only way to grow
is straight fearward...

VALUE REALM	CORE PERSONALITY	RELATIONSHIP FOCUS
Tends to look to objective values for responsibility		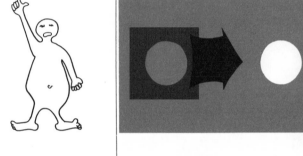
Tends to look to conceptual values for responsibility		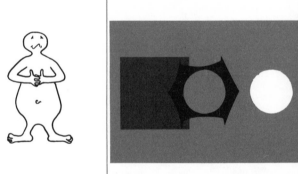
Tends to synthesize objective, conceptual and operational values for responsibility		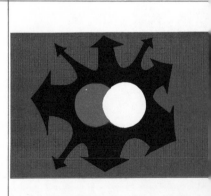

CONSCIOUSNESS LEVEL	
PURITAN ETHIC 	The first consciousness level is that of the Puritan forefathers whose allegiance was to the ethic of higher authority. Values were clear and specific. Born of the oppression of Europe and fired with the zealotry of the pioneer, this consciousness was loyal to the outside influence of the church and wrote the newly emerging laws in the same mode. Control and discipline were important. Knowledge was specific and consistent with the mandated ethic of higher authority.
TECHNOCRATIC ETHIC 	The second consciousness level is that of allegiance to the production-focused processes of the industrial revolution. The wealth of natural resources and men focused on cooperative management created an industrial complex whose lifeblood was growth, profit, and efficiency. Because managed cooperation was so important, dependency, mutuality, and consensus tended to prevail. The ethic of the team dominated. The procedural relationships that governed human involvement were perfected. Process became the core of the technocratic ethic.
INDIVIDUAL ETHIC 	The third consciousness level has the premises of the other two being evaluated by the individual. Each human is operationally assessing the other ethics. This puts the individual in control of the ethic rather than the ethic in control of the individual. Those who subscribe to Consciousness I and II are vociferous in their denouncement. It shifts from the then immutable power of ethical propriety to the individual. It is new but it is real. It stresses intrinsic-integrative functions as the manifestation of the ethic.

It is not important to argue the merits of the shift from the Puritan to the technocratic to the intrinsic ethic. It is instead important to recognize that it *has* begun and that it is a tendency that is growing.

The motivational ecology in which humans in the United States exist is rapidly becoming one in which independence, growth, and intrinsic freedom are extremely high priorities. With four-day work weeks and higher standards of living imminent, external stimuli will no longer suffice to distract or divert the growing awareness that the number of automobiles and television sets is a poor substitute for a viable, growing self.

The true counterculture movement is hardly discernible. Long hair and bellbottom pants are only symptomatic of the true changes taking place. Because this image of the counter culture *is* symptomatic, it is easily faked. The true changes are taking place quietly inside individuals who are spread from the halls of Harvard to the corridors of IBM to the furrowed lettuce fields of California.

Humans are beginning to realize the tremendous power of self. They can ignore the seduction of Madison Avenue or represent a social cause without aiming for notoriety. They go to church without trying to proselytize. They vote without coercion of their friends. They paint and write for joy. They love themselves but care for others. They live a mission but it is first and foremost an inner mission.

If I have been a prisoner
and a slave . . . if I have been ridiculed
and demeaned and you give me
                        your presence,
                        I will fear you.

If I have known guidance
and care . . . if I have been encouraged
and helped and you give me
                        your presence,
                        I will love you.

As I get to know myself
I find beauty in the mists of loneliness
that drift across my life.
Once I feared and avoided loneliness . . .
now I use it to help me know myself better.
I have found that I am the one who chooses whether
to see the clouds or the sun.
When loneliness comes now, I step inside myself
instead of going outside.
I focus on my presence instead of your absence.
I am beginning to realize not only how important you are

Just as the social warrior Pogo said, "We have met the enemy and he is us," and just as the scientist who discovered the missing link between anthropoid apes and civilized man claimed when he said "it's us," we say to you and ourselves that there has never been a time when such total potential was in the hands of so many. Each of us can grow since we each have the control in our own being. In addition, this inner growth allows us to move away from inhibiting others from growing. If I learn to care about myself in a real and growing way, it insures that I can care about you. No one likes to lose control and a person who has it cannot lose it. If I invest my power in things outside myself, I am forever attached to them by puppet strings. But if I invest my power in myself, then I can and will choose things outside me to love, to nourish, and to be loyal to.

I want to be in the presence
of humans who are free.
Free to accept me,
free to reject me,
free to ignore me,
because only then will I know
the meaning
instead of the shadows
of love
of life
and of me.

thanks .....
for letting us share
our journey with you —

Bob Samples
Bob Wohlford

BOB SAMPLES, the author-artist of this book, graduated from the University of Colorado intending to pursue a career in geology and geophysics. But one summer in west Texas on a geophysical exploration crew settled that idea. For the next few years, he worked at several museums in California and Colorado, received his M. Ed. at University of Colorado, and taught in a school district near Denver.

Then, with inputs from Jerome Bruner, David Hawkins, and Robert Burden, Bob began focusing his attention on what was to become a vocation—developing a more humane and creative approach to education and to life. After working with various curriculum projets, Bob started his own—the Environmental

Studies for Urban Youth Project. Funded by the National Science Foundation, this project created interdisciplinary curriculum materials, commercially called *Essence* cards, in tune with humanistic education. Now he is director of ESSENTIA, an NSF funded teaching-learning project at Evergreen State College in Olympia, Washington. Among other things, the project helps teachers use the *Essence* cards in their classrooms.

Bob travels the world lecturing and consulting in humanistic psychology and education. He has participated in the production of several prize-winning films, and his articles have appeared in *Human Behavior, Learning Magazine,* and *Media and Methods.* Currently, he is working on several books, including a novel and a book about human motivation called *The Metaphoric Mind.*

BOB WOHLFORD, the artist-author of this book, has been involved in creative communication all his life. He graduated from the University of Denver with a degree in commercial art, then did graduate work at the University of Denver, the University of Northern Colorado, and the University of Hawaii, where he received his M. Ed. in Educational Communications.

For 13 years, Bob worked with the Jefferson County, Colorado Schools as art teacher, Supervisor of Printing and Publications, graphic artist for the Instructional Materials Center, and Educational Media Specialist. Also, he has worked as an art instructor at Loretto Heights College in Denver.

Bob has facilitated numerous humanistic educational workshops for school districts and national educational conventions. He has also served as consultant and guest lecturer for several universities.

He has worked with the Environmental Studies Project since 1970, and now lives in Olympia, Washington, where he is Director of Media Development for ESSENTIA.

147

the others

It is awkward to try to thank a lifetime full of people for the insight (or lack of it) shown in my trying to write a book.

For ideas and concepts I must thank first Dorothy Sherman, then a professor of educational psychology at the University of Colorado, who early on confessed a distrust of psychologists who ignored people in their work. Then came Jerome Bruner, David Hawkins, W. J. J. Gordon, Robert Burden, and Margaret Donaldson, all of whom had time in their work with me in a couple of hot Cambridge summers to treat this naive explorer as a human. Then along came Jones (Dick) and a decade-long friendship replete with encouragement and chastisements, but mostly warmed with a glowing kind of honesty.

For love and living the list would include my former wife Chris, Carol Sink, Carol Garrison, John Thompson, Bob Lepper, Carol Roslund, Lucy Powell, Vicki Vandever, Gail Griffith, Bill Romey, Suzi Peters, Dot Curtis, Jim Lakis, Jack Carter, Nick Helburn, my parents Jean and Eve Thrall, Ray Bisque, Charline Breeden, Larry Watts, Bob Silber, Diane Caw, Kathy Saltzman, Noni Walker . . . and those so important . . . I forgot to remember them.

In the special category of those who made this book a reality, physically and with special skills that still bewilder me, I would include Marion Gilliam, Nancy Vickery, Tom Wohlford, Joyce Schaufenbuel, and certainly the Addison-Wesley staff.

148

The list closes with both anonymity and specificity . . . a double thousand teachers and students who suffered through workshops, classes, picnics, field trips, and all that goes with the classroom. And the thousand people who took the time to talk in bars, beaches, mountains, airplanes, and alleys. And the shadowy though significant people who drift in and out of focus when memory ruffles feathers that now seem at rest. And finally to those very real people who build special banks of thought and feeling in my world right now, Cheryl Charles, Bob Wohlford, and my four-year-old philosopher-therapist Kari Peters.

Thanks.

Bob Samples

acknowledgements

p. 6   O. J. Harvey, Psychology Department, University
              of Colorado, Boulder, Colorado 80302. Author
              of numerous books and articles.

p. 17   Frederick S. Perls, from *Gestaslt Therapy Verba-
              tim* © 1969 Real People Press.

p. 23   Colin Wilson, *New Pathways in Psychology,*
              New York, Taplinger, 1972, p.67.

p. 24–25   Carl Rogers, *Journal of Abnormal and Social Psy-
              chology,* "Toward a Modern Approach to Values:
              The Valuing Process in the Mature Person,"
              1964, V. 68, No. 2, pp. 160–67.

p. 30   Gordon Allport, *The Nature of Prejudice,* New
              York, Doubleday, 1958, p. 157.

p. 38   S. Freud, General reference to approaches to
              creativity.

p. 40   Henri Rousseau: *The Sleeping Gypsy* 1897. The
              Museum of Modern Art, New York; gift of Mrs.
              Simon Guggenheim.

p. 42   Song title, "A Dream is a Wish your Heart
              Makes," Walt Disney Productions, "Cinderella."

p. 42   Lawrence Kubie, *Neurotic Distortion of the Crea-
              tive Process,* Noonday, 1958/1961.

p. 42   Richard Jones, *Fantasy and Feeling in Education,* New York, New York University Press, 1968, and *The New Psychology of Dreaming,* New York, Grune & Stratton, 1970.

p. 44–45   Jerome Butler, *Essays for the Left Hand,* Cambridge, Belknap Press of Harvard University Press, 1963, p. 18.

p. 45   Albert Einstein, Rotunda of the Jefferson County Planetarium.

p. 46–48   Lawrence Kubie, *Neurotic Distortion of the Creative Process,* Noonday, p. 40.

p. 47   Robert Ornstein, *The Psychology of Consciousness,* New York, Viking Press, 1972.

p. 59   T. Roczak, *The Making of the Counter Culture,* New York, Doubeday, 1969, p. 222.

p. 106   A. Maslow, *Toward a Psychology of Being,* New York, Van Nostrand Reinhold, 1968, p. 46–47.

p. 127   State Law on acccountability. Ten Commandments from the Bible.

p. 129   P. L. Berger, *Invitation to Sociology,* New York, Doubleday, 1963, pp. 10–11.

p. 130   American Geological Institute, *Essence I* and *II* Teacher's Guide, Menlo Park, Calif.: Addison-Wesley, 1975.

p. 131   *The Good Times Are Comin'* (By: Hal David and John Barry) Copyright © 1970 by April Music, Inc., Barwin Music Inc. & J. C. Music Co. All Rights Reserved.

p. 139   C. Reich, *The Greening of America,* Random House, 1970.

p. 143   Walt Kelly, "Pogo," New York, Simon and Schuster, Inc.

Illustration Acknowledgments

All photos by Bob Samples, except pp. 77, 146 Suzi Peters; p. 131 Lucy Powell; p. 24 Bruce Anderson "Mirror," p. 141 a painting by Bob Samples.